SECRETS OF
FACE-*to*-FACE
COMMUNICATION

HOW TO COMMUNICATE WITH POWER

**Peter Urs Bender
Dr. Robert A. Tracz**

Stoddart

Published in 2001 by Stoddart Publishing Co. Limited
895 Don Mills Road, 400-2 Park Centre, Toronto, Canada M3C 1W3

Distributed in Canada by:
General Distribution Services Ltd.
325 Humber College Blvd., Toronto, Ontario M9W 7C3
Tel. (416) 213-1919   Fax (416) 213-1917
Email cservice@genpub.com

Distributed in the United States by:
General Distribution Services Inc.
PMB 128, 4500 Witmer Industrial Estates, Niagara Falls, New York 14305-1386
Toll-free Tel. 1-800-805-1083   Toll-free Fax 1-800-481-6207
Email gdsinc@genpub.com

05   04   03   02   01   1   2   3   4   5

CANADIAN CATALOGUING IN PUBLICATION DATA

Bender, Peter Urs, 1944–
Secrets of face-to-face communication: how to communicate with power

ISBN 0-7737-6184-5

1. Communication in management. I. Tracz, Robert A., 1951–. II. Title.
HD30.3.B46 2001   658.4'5   C00-932844-0

U.S. CATALOGING-IN-PUBLICATION DATA
(Library of Congress Standards)
Bender, Peter Urs.
Secrets of face-to-face communication: how to communicate with power /
Peter Urs Bender and Robert Tracz. — 1st ed.
[256] p. ; ill. : cm.
ISBN: 0-7737-61845 (pbk.)
1. Business communication. 2. Communicative competence.
3. Oral communication. I. Tracz, Robert. II. Title.
658.452 21 2001 CIP

Cover Design: Rod Frost Design
Text Design: Tannice Goddard

*We acknowledge for their financial support of our
publishing program the Canada Council, the Ontario Arts
Council, and the Government of Canada through the
Book Publishing Industry Development Program (BPIDP).*

THE CANADA COUNCIL | LE CONSEIL DES ARTS
FOR THE ARTS | DU CANADA
SINCE 1917 | DEPUIS 1957

Visit the web site www.SecretsofFacetoFaceCommunication.com
Printed and bound in Canada

| CONTENTS

| PREFACE

Secrets of Face-to-Face Communication is first and foremost a *system*. It is a system based on experience — the experience of Peter Urs Bender and Dr. Robert Tracz. We are two very different individuals who, nevertheless, are communication specialists. In this book we try to give you, our reader, clear, crisp, down-to-earth guidance on how to improve communication with anyone you deal with.

The book most emphatically does *not* outline a philosophy or way of life — other than to support the objective of improved communication with others. It most certainly is not a psychological treatise — although those of you familiar with psychology may notice that some of its techniques refer to modern research as it has been absorbed into popular culture. For these reasons you will not find a footnoted tome that acknowledges every source for every idea page by page. We willingly, however, acknowledge our debt to those who have helped us along the way in our *Recommended Reading* section on page 231.

What you will find here is a system based on experience — our own experience and that of others. We emphasize the "system" aspect of this book because we know from our other work that *systematizing* your approach to virtually any activity — marketing, presenting, leading — can help you excel at it. In fact, we believe that face-to-face communication is one of the most important and fulfilling activities humans can accomplish — but like any activity, it needs to acquire some conscious structure in order for you to proceed with success.

From the day we are born, we begin to communicate. In fact, it's true to say that you cannot *not* communicate. Poor communication skills can condemn you to a life of mediocrity and unhappiness. However, good communication skills can lead you to success beyond your wildest dreams.

By the time we reach adulthood, most of our communication activities are performed subconsciously — that is, we use our communication skills whether we are aware of them or not. This book will help make you more conscious of how you communicate and how you can change your style to become a better communicator.

You will notice some similarities between this and other books that have appeared, specifically under Peter Urs Bender's authorship, because the topics here and in Peter's other books are interconnected. *Leadership from Within,* for instance, urges us to get to know our inner selves and to call on the inner strengths we all have but might not be aware of.

Secrets of Power Presentations and *Secrets of Power Marketing* are both about acquiring skills to make us more successful in life. That's what *Secrets of Face-to-Face Communication* is all about, too. It's a manual about acquiring the skills to make you a better communicator. It will also help you to be more successful in dealing with people in your personal and working lives.

Peter Urs Bender
Dr. Robert A. Tracz

| THANK YOU

*S*ecrets of *Power Presentations,* my first book, was created by myself and Michael McClintock and edited by my wife, Frances, long ago in 1991. Today it is published in many languages, available internationally, and is required reading in many top companies.

Leadership from Within, my second book, would never have reached the shelves if Eric Hellman had not been born. It, too, became an international bestseller.

Secrets of Power Marketing, my third book, was the work of myself and my first licensee, George Torok. It hit the bestseller lists in Canada on its first printing, and is also well on its way to international fame.

This book, *Secrets of Face-to-Face Communication,* was the brainchild of Dr. Robert Tracz, a very talented speaker and outstanding trainer. I had lunch with him one day, and he convinced me he had a book to write with me. We encountered some problems in the initial writing and recruited the very capable help of my assistant, George Hancocks. George had faith in the ideas and the manuscript right from the start. He took our original work and revamped it into the format you now see. I would like to thank him for his tireless effort in helping us pull this project together.

So I want to make it perfectly clear, in case I am ever nominated for the Nobel Prize for English Literature. I will not accept it. I didn't write this book alone. It was created with the help of many other smart individuals. The ideas are Bob Tracz's and mine. But again, I have to say that we got most of them from somewhere else. I think there is nothing new under the sun — it's just presented differently.

But most of all, without you, gentle reader, none of my books would ever have been bought! Publishing is easy: selling is tough! Thanks for all your feedback, for telling others what my books have done for you. Thanks to your recommendations, I can keep on creating books with others! As a matter of fact, keep your eyes open for my next work together with George Hancocks. It's not for you but for the "tweens" around you. We call it *The Bug in You!*

Peter Urs Bender

There is no such thing as good writing! There is only good rewriting. I've learned that if you choose good people to collaborate with, you will ease the rewriting process considerably.

In many ways, writing acknowledgements is the most difficult part. What if I forget to mention someone? There are so many to thank.

I'm indebted to each of the following people:

Peter Urs Bender, author, speaker, and trainer extraordinaire. He simplifies the complicated.

George Hancocks, writer. Without his contribution, this book would not flow as smoothly as it now does.

Marnie Kramarich, Gillian Watts, Jennifer Warren, and others. These exceptional editors persevered and guided us through the writing/rewriting process. Their suggestions improved the book considerably.

And finally, I would like to thank Don Bastian and Stoddart Publishing for their suggestions and belief in the project.

Many others — authors, speakers, seminar participants, and friends — added their knowledge, advice, and expertise to enrich the ideas within this book. I'm indebted to each of them.

And finally, I'd like to thank you, the reader, for buying and reading this book. These ideas have been collected and passed on in the hope that you will incorporate them into your daily life. You will improve your ability to understand and to be understood. Better understanding is the key to improved relationships and effectiveness.

Dr. Robert A. Tracz

A NOTE
TO READERS

*S*ecrets of Face-to-Face Communication is presented in an alphabetical style to make it easier for you to access key concepts. Nevertheless, sections that are related to each other are clearly marked with bracketed comments, like this: (see *Preface*). By following these italicized markers, you can delve deeper into the topic in which you are interested, or into topics that are closely related.

This is really a book about "one-on-one" communication. When you are communicating with another individual, you are in a short-term partnership with that person. Hence we use the term "communication partner," or often just "partner," to designate that person. The word "partner" also has the advantage of being a neutral term. It can apply to either men or women.

Occasionally, and for variation, we describe our partners as "he" or "she," and sometimes when we get stuck, we fall back on the old "he or she." We tried throughout to be gender-conscious in our language. By the time we finished, we felt we had the balance about right. We certainly hope you will feel this is a book about communicating with other human beings, whatever their gender, and we hope our use of the masculine and feminine pronouns, where appropriate, meets with your approval.

SECRETS OF
FACE-*to*-FACE
COMMUNICATION

ACTION CYCLE

The first step east is the first step west.
— ZEN PROVERB

The first action in any communication is to clearly outline your communication objective. It's important for you to understand clearly what it is you want so that you can more clearly explain it to your partner. Once you have done this, you must move into the action cycle. Think of it simply as *act, aware,* and *adjust*. But first, know what you want.

1. *Act* on it.
2. Be *aware* of the immediate results.
3. *Adjust* your actions if you're not getting what you want.

Let's go into this a bit further. *Act* on your objective, taking the best action you can given your present state of knowledge. Then, be *aware* of the outcome by establishing a rapport with your partner — observing, speaking, and listening. The awareness of that outcome is the basis for your next action, which you will *adjust* accordingly. Focus, act, observe, and adjust again. Continue the communication action cycle until you succeed or exhaust your options.

You must be flexible and adapt to your partner's style and the situation. Remember that if you aren't getting the results you want, you need to change your approach. Ask yourself again: Do I know what I want to achieve? You must make sure the messages you're sending are the messages you intend to send. You must also be sure the message that's received by your partner is the same as the message you sent.

THE CYCLE OF NATURE

When I was a little boy, I remember the teacher telling us about the clouds, the water, and the rain. Rain falls to the ground, seeps through the earth, and ends up in streams and rivers. Rivers flow into the sea where the heat from the sun evaporates the water, and the cycle begins again. Nothing has changed . . . It's our responsibility as adults to find, identify, and act on all the mysterious cycles we encounter in our lives.

— Peter

ACTIVE LISTENING

When you know why you're listening, you know what you're listening for.
— ROBERT

The average rate of speech is about 150 words a minute. The average rate of hearing is about 500 to 750 words a minute. Not only can you hear faster than your partner can speak, you have the potential to project what he may be going to say — and so become bored.

Because you're anxious to speed up the conversation, you stop listening effectively. Active listening skills help you focus on what your partner's saying.

You need to do three things to listen actively:

1. Listen with *HEART*.
2. Avoid roadblocks.
3. Listen holistically.

HEART is an acronym for active listening. Have you ever noticed the word "ear" in the word "hear" in the word "heart"? It's not an accident. The key to understanding is to listen with your heart. Listening is a gift

— one you give from the heart.

H   *Hush*
E   *Empathize before you evaluate*
A   *Ask questions and attend*
R   *Reflect and paraphrase*
T   *Tone*

Hush means just what it says. Stop talking and focus on the speaker and the message (see *Distractions*).

Empathize before you evaluate means that you should listen for your partner's feelings, then evaluate the facts that support them (see *Empathy*).

Ask questions, again, means just that. Be there for your partner. In other words, *attend* to your partner, listening intently and demonstrating that you are, in fact, listening (see *Attention*).

Reflect and paraphrase is another way of demonstrating interest (see *Reflecting*).

Tone means that you should listen to your partner's tone. It will tell as much as, or more than, their words alone will (see *Tone*).

When was the last time you were listening to someone with half an ear, and then were suddenly asked a pertinent question? If you are truly unflappable, you might have replied with a cool "Would you mind repeating the question please? I didn't quite understand." More likely, you would simply be embarrassed, stammer some silly reply, and confirm in the speaker's mind that you had truly not been listening. Listening is an active state, and your partner knows immediately if you are not participating. It's important to allow your partner to see that you're listening.

LISTENING CAN BRING BENEFITS

I bought a cottage from a professor who was fascinated with Greek mythology. During my school days, I think I missed those classes. However, before we closed the deal, he invited me to visit him to have dinner. Before I went I looked in my books, and found a few buzzwords about mythology. During dinner I threw them out to see what would happen. He started to talk, and never stopped. I couldn't do anything but listen — first, because I didn't understand the subject, and second, because he didn't stop talking. When I left he told me it had been one of the most enjoyable dinner conversations he'd ever had. The result? He threw in lots of extras to the deal, because he thought that anyone who likes Greek mythology is a person on his own wavelength, which means he's a good guy!

— Peter

THE AMIABLE

Let's work together!

There are four broad behavioral styles that allow us to determine the way a person is behaving at any moment. They also give us the ability to respond appropriately to a person's actions. These four styles are briefly outlined in *Differences*. Here is more on one of those styles.

Devoted, consistent, dependable, and loyal, the Amiable is a hard worker and will persevere long after others have given up. He or she is a team player, cooperative and easy to get along with, trustful, sensitive, and a good listener. Working in groups with cooperative individuals, the Amiable tries to avoid confrontation. He or she enjoys company, performs best in a stable environment, and often has a stabilizing effect on others.

Weaknesses include indecision and an inability to take risks. Amiables are often too focused on others, conforming, quiet, and passive. They often won't speak up for themselves, are too compliant and nice, and often painstakingly slow to make decisions.

The Amiable's pleasure is stability and cooperation. Her pain is change and chaos.

When communicating with an Amiable

— Be relaxed and agreeable
— Maintain the status quo
— Be logical and systematic
— Create a plan with written guidelines
— Be prepared to answer "why" questions
— Be predictable
— Agree clearly and often
— Use the word "we"
— Don't push
— Don't rush
— Compliment him or her as a team player
— Be a good listener

THE AMIABLE . . . PORTRAIT OF AN OFFICE

The first thing you will notice in the Amiable's office will be pictures of loved ones on the desk: husband, wife, family, favorite pets. They'll be in a candid style, and the Amiable loves to talk about them. On the walls will be colorful photos of landscapes, waterfalls, birds, and sunsets. You'll find flowers or plants that are growing well and office colors that are harmonious and restful. The person will almost certainly be dressed in colors that match. Furniture will be fashionable, but not overwhelming. Files are present, but usually kept out of the way. If you're a little late, the Amiable won't mind. If you have the Amiable in your company, he or she will stay with you. The Amiable likes company newsletters, picnics, gatherings, and retirement parties. *Symbol:* Dove.

— Peter

THE
ANALYTICAL

Think it through.

This is another of the four broad behavioral styles described in *Differences*. Recognizing any of these styles enables us to respond appropriately to the actions of these individuals.

The Analytical is polite but reserved, logical, fact-oriented, and task-oriented. This person's focus is on precision and perfection. Other strengths include persistence, diligence, caution, and a systematic approach.

Weaknesses involve being withdrawn, boring, quiet, reclusive, and even sullen at times. If he or she seems indecisive, it's because of a need to assess all the data. Perfectionism can be a fault if the Analytical pushes it too far. This person is definitely not a risk-taker.

The Analytical needs to be right, and won't openly discuss ideas until confident in a decision. Her pleasure is accuracy; her pain is to be wrong and criticized.

When communicating with an Analytical

— Be systematic, thorough, deliberate, and precise

— Focus on the task

— Be prepared to answer many "how" questions

— Provide analysis and facts

— Don't get too personal

— Recognize and acknowledge the need to be accurate and logical

— Don't rush unnecessarily

— Expect to repeat yourself

— Allow time for evaluation

— Use lots of evidence

— Compliment the precision and accuracy of the completed work

THE ANALYTICAL . . . PORTRAIT OF AN OFFICE

The first thing you notice will probably be the glasses. The Analytical will have worn out his or her eyes from constantly reading everything. On the wall you may see a framed degree, but the chief decoration will be charts, figures, and graphs of every kind. The Analytical is not very friendly, will often greet you skeptically, and doesn't want to share much — especially anything personal. There will be no flowers or plants; for the Analytical, they belong in greenhouses. On the desk will be only business-related information, and that will be carefully arranged. It's not a power office, but it definitely will be functional. As for color, black and white will do nicely. *Symbol:* Owl.

— **Peter**

ANSWERS

*Responding to questions clearly, confidently,
and gracefully is an art.*
— ROBERT

The key to answering questions is organized thinking.
Properly answered questions clarify confusing situations, or buy you time
to think of an answer. They can also soften hard feelings and provide
additional food for thought.

Whatever the case, it's important that your answer makes you appear
organized and intelligent. It's also important to answer the question and
not offer more information that you're asked for. There are many ways to
organize your reply, as well as to organize your thoughts while thinking
on your feet. Here are ten ways to organize your answers:

1. USING HISTORICAL OR CHRONOLOGICAL ORDER
    In this approach, ask yourself, "What happened first? What fol-
    lowed?" You could answer by discussing the problem from the
    perspective of the past, present, and future. Follow the natural
    sequence of events as they occurred.

    For instance, if you were in an accident, you would state the direction you were traveling in, followed by your first indication that something was wrong. You would continue to relive the event moment to moment as it happened to you, in the exact sequence in which it occurred, until you completed your reply.

2. GOING FROM MOST IMPORTANT TO LEAST IMPORTANT
This approach forces you to prioritize. To accomplish this, zero in on the key issue. Then move to the next most important issue, then to the third, and so on. Prioritize each issue with regard to importance and itemize your points.

For instance, you could state that there are three things you should know about the topic.
The first is . . .
The second is . . .
The third is . . .

Don't go into too much detail initially. See if your listener remains interested. Begin by stating your opinion or conclusion. Then list the main points of your answer and go on to elaborate on the details. Give an example. Finally, restate your opinion or conclusion. Think of it in the words of the salesman's creed: "First you tell 'em you're gonna tell 'em; then you tell 'em; then you tell 'em you've told 'em."

3. FRAMING YOUR ANSWER
A *frame* consists of a powerful anchor, the benefits of your plan, and how they could apply to what you're talking about.

Imagine trying to convince someone of the value of using an accountant to do an income tax return instead of doing it on his or her own. It might go like this:

"I can appreciate your concern at spending the extra money. I was concerned, too, when I first went to an accountant. I couldn't justify the expense. But it turned out the accountant found several things I had missed, including an additional $2,000 return. That was more than twice his fee. I've used an accountant ever since.

"Sometimes the value of a service is hidden. The benefits of my proposal are . . . You may not have realized this, but . . . You will likely spend twice as much subcontracting the work out to other sources, not to mention the investment of your time. With an accountant, you could use his service on an ongoing basis at a saving of . . . You will also have the added benefit of an accountant saving you many headaches and worries. What would that peace of mind be worth to you?"

The *anchor* is the story of the accountant to drive home your point. An anchor might be a story, anecdote, statistic, quote, or anything you can think of to make your point.

After you have provided an answer, list several *benefits*. Benefits are not features. They list what you have determined to be important to the person you're talking to. In this example, the information about subcontracting and savings comprises the benefits.

Then help the person realize how the accountant's services will help them, while adding *hidden benefits* or other things they might not be aware of. In this example, the hidden benefits may be that hiring an accountant will save the person headaches and worries.

Finally, as in the example, conclude with a question to mentally involve them and stimulate their thinking.

4. USING "FEEL, FELT, FOUND"

This question-answering technique is useful for persuading people to your way of thinking and for addressing their concerns. Start by acknowledging their comments, and then proceed to improve their understanding.

It might go like this:

"That's interesting. A lot of people *feel* that way about . . . "

"I *felt* the same way as well, until I realized that . . . "

"What I have *found* to work well is . . . "

5. REVERSING OR RELAYING

Here you may choose to *reverse* the question back to the questioner, or even to *relay* it for someone else to answer. In reversing the question you might say, "That's an interesting question. How would you answer that?"

In a relayed question you might say, "That's an interesting question. What do you think about that, Terry?" or "Does anyone have any thoughts or other views on that?"

6. SETTING YOUR BOUNDARIES

If you don't feel comfortable answering a question fully, establish at the outset what part of the question you *are* going to answer. Then, answer by focusing on only one part of the issue. You might even use this technique to let the speaker know what questions are not welcome, or even justified.

7. ACKNOWLEDGING YOU DON'T KNOW

If you really don't know the answer to the question you're being asked, the first thing to do is buy some time by asking for clarification. If you still don't know the answer, don't fake it. Admit you don't know and offer to get back when you do. If you make the promise to get back to them, make sure you do.

8. OBSCURING THE ANSWER

If you want to avoid a direct question, answer indirectly. Do this by giving multiple possibilities in your answer, or maybe even being sufficiently vague in your reply to convey the idea that you have actually answered the question. You would then bridge from the question to where you want to go — this lets you change the subject and topic without your listener perhaps even realizing what you've done.

Several other obscuring techniques involve

- Questioning the intent behind the question
- Addressing any underlying assumptions you detect in the question
- Reinterpreting the question by saying, "As I understand your question . . . " and then answering according to your interpretation
- Using a disarming comment to deflect the question

ANSWERS

- Tactfully changing the subject

9. USING HUMOR

Answer questions you want to avoid with a joke, an anecdote, or a noncommittal answer. Humor can get you into trouble, but if you're in trouble, humor can get you out.

10. ADMITTING YOU'RE WRONG

When you're questioned about something you've said or done and you know you are wrong, admit it — quickly and emphatically. This will usually defuse further discussion and questioning. If you try to hide the mistake, however, your partner may pursue it relentlessly, and you will lose your integrity in the process.

By the same token, don't belittle yourself. Everyone makes mistakes — even you. Don't make excuses. Consider explaining what you have learned from the experience. We all grow and learn like this.

THE RIGHT ANSWER

I was with the president and a group of vice presidents from my company, all eager beavers and ready for battle, and the president asked me what I thought on a certain topic of interest. I knew that the VPs were waiting to pounce on me if I said anything at all. In my mind I had an answer, but I knew that if I gave it, it could embarrass both me and the company president. I thought for a moment, and then replied, "I can't give you an immediate answer because I don't know enough about the situation." It was a sidestep, but the president smiled at me approvingly and said, "Good. You know how to defuse the mines."

— Peter

14   BENDER/TRACZ

APOLOGIZING

Never make a defence or apology
before you be accused.
— KING CHARLES I

We make mistakes; we're human. Admit it quickly, wholeheartedly, and adamantly. Apology eases our minds, calms someone who feels hard done by, and can even save our relationships. What if, however, we're not at fault? Well, an apology might still be in order. Your strategy will change depending on the degree of severity of the situation.

Reasons for the situation aren't always necessary. In fact, they may make you feel better, but they rarely help your cause. The person feeling slighted often interprets them, at best, as excuses. Or, they could interpret it in the worst way possible: as you telling them they are less important than what happened. Either interpretation is a no-win situation.

The exception to this rule is any reason based on extraordinary circumstances. Most people readily accept things beyond your control, such as a fire in the office, having to drive your spouse to the hospital in an emergency, or an unexpected death. Less pertinent reasons are viewed as excuses.

To find forgiveness, follow the 8 A's.

— *Agree* wholeheartedly if you're wrong and *Accept* responsibility for your actions

— *Acknowledge* their concerns if you're not in the wrong

— *Apologize* for something, even if it's only for their confusion

— *Avoid* making excuses and offering reasons unless they happen to be of an extraordinary nature

— Tell them what *Actions* you're going to take to help them to make it right or to prevent these circumstances from happening again.

— Give them control by offering suggestions for their *Approval*

— Tell them you *Appreciate* their bringing this to your attention if it's appropriate

THE MISSED APPOINTMENT

We miss appointments. Failing to call in advance is rude, yet it happens. How you handle it will determine whether your relationship will remain healthy or be strained.

This happened to me. I was to meet my most important prospect client for lunch — or so I thought, since I had written in twelve noon and a restaurant name. In actual fact, the meeting was to be in her office.

I called as soon as I became aware of my oversight, adamantly apologized, and accepted full responsibility. I acknowledged how frustrating waiting in her office must have been, offered to treat her to lunch at her convenience, and suggested two times for her approval. I assured her this was the exception and not the rule and thanked her for being so understanding.

Our relationship survived and we now can laugh about that first meeting.

— Robert

APPEARANCE

Don't judge a book by its cover.
Beauty is only skin deep, but ugliness goes down
to the bone.
— TRADITIONAL SAYINGS

When taken together with other pieces of information, appearance will tell a lot about a person's emotional or mental state. It will also indicate how an individual feels about himself or herself. Someone who looks grubby, for instance, may lack self-esteem.

When meeting with a partner, watch for these things:

— How is your partner dressed?
— In what condition is your partner's hair?
— Does your partner look tired or refreshed?
— Is your partner's image consistent with his or her profession or status?
— Does your partner appear trustworthy and credible?

THE SATURDAY SUIT

I used to have what I called a "Saturday suit," which I kept only for weekends when I went out shopping. The reason is simple. I found that if I looked well-dressed when I went into a store, I got more courteous attention. Perhaps it's not so important to wear a suit these days, because dress has become much more casual. But try it for yourself. Wear a suit or "dress-up" clothes when you visit the stores and see how much more likely you are to get served quickly.

— **Peter**

ASKING QUESTIONS

Questions, asked sincerely and tactfully, indicate to your partner that you are listening and seriously considering their ideas.
— ROBERT

The easiest way to learn about someone and their ideas is to ask them. But remember, people are sometimes reluctant to talk about themselves. To get them going, it's important to be tactful and non-threatening.

It's also important to remember to give them time to answer. If you need a guideline, count up to eight (using the old "thousand, thousand-and-one" method) to give them time to consider their ideas and formulate an answer.

Show them respect. Help by asking only a single question at a time. State your question clearly so it's easy to answer. Listen closely to the answer and restate it in your own words to be sure you understand the reply.

Use the following four steps when you ask a question:

1. Have a purpose
2. Create a safe environment

3. Use the floodlight/spotlight approach
4. Listen actively

HAVE A PURPOSE

Stop what you're doing and focus. Know why you're asking the question, because it's related to what you want from the conversation.

— What do you want to achieve by asking the question?
— Where do you want to go with the conversation?
— What is your final objective?
— Do you want specific information?
— Do you want general information?
— Do you want to establish rapport?
— Do you want to offer or gain support?
— Do you simply want to enjoy a conversation?
— Do you want to implant ideas or influence the decision?
— Do you want to understand the person and his ideas better?

Your approach to asking questions depends on what you currently know and understand (or think you know and understand), and where you want to be (or think you want to be) when you're done. It's important to remain flexible and open. You may think you understand someone, but ask for clarification anyway. You want to hear them explain it in their own way. Maybe they've discovered something you didn't know or understand. At the very least you'll discover what they know, think, and feel.

CREATE A SAFE ENVIRONMENT

Choose a style of communication that is appropriate to your listener's own style. Ask your questions in a non-threatening manner. Both are important to establish and maintain rapport.

Create an environment of mutually supportive communication. Make it safe and non-threatening for them to respond. Don't interrogate. Be willing to share information about yourself. This is true two-way communication.

We respond to someone in the same way we're spoken to. Have you noticed, for instance, that you tend to speak with an accent when you spend time with someone with an accent? Have you ever become enthusiastic while sitting next to an enthusiastic person, or apathetic when sitting next to someone apathetic?

You need to be sincere, interested, and helpful while you ask questions. The responses you get are at least partly determined by how you ask. Think adult-to-adult. Once you start to sound like a scolding parent or a whining child, the other person will clam up, rebel, or become defensive.

Mirror the other person (see *Matching*). Match their rate of speech, gestures, and key words (see *Key Words*). Be observant (see *Observing: What to Look For*). Communication requires lots of give and take.

If necessary, ask for permission to ask questions. It's essential to establish mutual trust. The quickest way to bring the conversation to a grinding halt is to make the other person defensive. All it takes is an accusing "Why did you?" or "How could you?" to stop everything. Be compassionate. Don't put your partner in the hot seat.

USE THE FLOODLIGHT/SPOTLIGHT APPROACH

This requires starting with the general, open questions, and then gradually moving in with more direct, closed questions. You may use this approach exclusively or partially, depending on your level of understanding or needs. See *Questions* for a more detailed explanation of how to use this tool.

LISTEN ACTIVELY

Listen carefully to your partner's answers as you probe further for greater understanding.

Normally, about 70 to 90 percent of what is said is misunderstood or filtered out, and only 25 percent of that is retained. This phenomenon is called "selective listening" and it can be a real barrier to understanding.

Why is so much of the message filtered out?

— Maybe there's no clear purpose behind it
— Maybe there's no motivation to listen
— Maybe you dislike the communicator's style
— Maybe one or both of you are tired
— Maybe you're not prepared to invest the emotional involvement necessary to listen actively
— Maybe you and your partner are experiencing distractions
— Maybe you don't like the message (or the speaker)

If you're under stress, the speaker might be as well. There are countless reasons why we don't listen. Nevertheless, it's still your responsibility to seek understanding, and listening actively is the key (see *Active Listening* for more).

Evaluate your partner's answer, as well as the emotion and feelings behind it. Relate it to what you already know. Evaluate as an ongoing process. Think of it as trimming the sail while maintaining your course. Then, evaluate again when the conversation is over. What would you do differently?

Probe for detailed information by helping the speaker communicate the message — but don't put words in his mouth, or finish thoughts for him. Discuss feelings and reasons. Really search for complete understanding.

Use open questions to draw out information. For example: "Please tell me more about _____ . What else is important to you? What bothers you about _____ ?"

Reflect their key ideas and words to ensure you have received the message correctly. Then paraphrase what you heard in your own words to ensure correct understanding. You may or may not agree with the message, but make sure you have understood it. Once the speaker's position is clear, you can state yours.

Finally, conclude by summarizing what you've both agreed on, to clear up any possible confusion, and ask, "Is there anything else we've missed? Have I made myself clear?"

ALWAYS ASK FIRST

When I was new to this country, I met a Nobel Prize-winner at a party. I had no knowledge of his subject — physics — in fact, I had failed physics in school. In my innocence I could only ask questions: how, why, what, when, where. I asked them all night long. The physicist enjoyed himself. He was talking about his prime topic — and I was off the hook. Later in life I learned that I was asking life-saving questions. They were so basic, they did not reveal my own ignorance.

— Peter

ASSUMPTIONS

Never assume a virtue if you know you haven't got it.
— P<small>ETER</small>

Assumptions will block understanding every time. All assumptions need to be shared between you and your partner to improve understanding. When you're the least bit doubtful, assuming understanding is dangerous. Why not buy time and clarify what someone means, especially if it's a stressful situation? Here's how to go about it:

1. Breathe — you need the oxygen
2. Maintain eye contact
3. Ask for clarification — "What do you mean?" — this buys time to think and provides you with more information
4. Listen carefully and respond briefly to your partner's main concern
5. Remain silent as you wait for your partner's response

What kinds of assumptions should we look for?

1. **Assumptions about your own knowledge and flexibility.** They can lead

to ultimatums and finality, e.g., "I'm the expert!" Listen for new and creative ideas. They can come from anyone at any time.

2. **Assumptions about the listener's responses and feelings.** By assuming how someone *may* act or feel, you close your mind to how they *do* act or feel. In effect, you will find evidence to support what you expect to find, and selectively eliminate other information.

3. **Assumptions about communication skills.** One of the biggest assumptions is that if you can hear, you can listen, and if you can speak, you can communicate. That creates the expectation that your partner understands the words you use, that no feedback is required, and that attitudes and the way in which something is said aren't important.

4. **Assumptions about people or the environment.** Some common examples: "I couldn't make a difference," or "I'm only one person," or "Nothing ever changes around here," or "Everyone does it." You've heard them all — maybe even from yourself.

THE WHITE SOCKS

When I first came to this country, I wanted to become a typical North American. I bought some white socks and some chewing gum and proceeded to Americanize myself. Then, one evening, I was taking a bus home and I noticed some Swiss tourists sitting opposite me. They were saying in their native Swiss tongue, "Look at that guy! He's a typical North American. Look at his white socks!" When I heard that and noticed that they thought I would not understand their comments, I became more blatant about flashing my socks and chewing my gum, and the more I did that, the more outrageous their comments became. Finally, the bus stopped to let me out. I smiled at them, and said in perfect Swiss-German with a smile on my face, "I hope you enjoy North America and us natives!" and exited without another word.

— Peter

ATTENTION

A pair of ears will drain a hundred tongues.
— BENJAMIN FRANKLIN

Paying attention is an important part of the *HEART* approach to active listening. The "A" in *HEART* stands for *ask* questions and *attend*. Paying attention is not only polite, it's the way to get what you need from your conversation partner.

Be there mentally and physically. Vocalization, facial gestures, and body language are all ways in which you can focus using non-verbal communication.

Vocalization includes words ("Oh really?" "Is that so?"), non-words ("mm-hmm"; "ahh"), and silence. They may not seem very potent, but they are excellent ways to demonstrate to your partner that you're listening and aware of the message.

Your most important facial gestures are eye contact and smiling. Both should feel and look natural. Try to be comfortable with silence, and give your partner the mental space that she or he needs to think.

Body language also needs to be comfortable and relaxed (see *Matching*). Your gestures should be reflective of your partner's. Using gestures that support and encourage him or her will also contribute to understanding.

One of the best ways of remembering how to "attend" is to use the *SOFTENERS* mnemonic.

S *mile* — occasionally and appropriately
O *pen your body posture* — face your partner
F *orward lean* — toward your partner
T *ouch* — be careful!
E *ye contact* — two to six seconds is the average range
N *odding* — and other actions that show you are listening
E *ncourage* — ask questions, use supportive vocalizations
R *eframe* — ask yourself, "How would I feel if that was me?"
S *pace* — about three feet

Paying attention will invite your partner to participate fully in the conversation. See *SOFTENERS* for more on this positive approach.

SHOW YOU'RE LISTENING

It's hard — in fact, almost impossible — to pay attention to someone when they're telling you something for your own good. They've got their nerve! Don't they realize you're busy with something else?

I remember a cartoon from a newspaper years ago. A small boy was trying to get his father, who was reading a newspaper, to pay attention to him. The son said, "Dad, you have to listen with your eyes, too." Isn't that true?

Perception, what you think is true, is true only for you. If you don't feel someone is listening to you, then — in your mind at least — he isn't. Even if he could repeat every word, you would still feel ignored. It's one thing to listen; it's another to show you're listening. People need to *see* you listen. Pay attention.

— **Robert**

ATTITUDE

You have no control over anyone but yourself.
— PETER

When you deal with another person, you must have a genuine desire and willingness to get along, no matter what. How you feel about your partner is determined by what you believe about that person. The opposite is also true. You need to create the feeling that you're positive, committed to working together, and flexible. Present yourself as relaxed, personable, and confident.

To get yourself into the right attitude, it helps to

- Move — motion changes emotion
- Read or think of affirmative statements (positive self-talk)
- Listen to some good music
- Listen to positive motivating tapes
- Use any device that works to coax yourself into concentration
- Imagine how you would feel if you were about to meet an old friend
- Get yourself into a state where you are

- Demonstrating concern and compassion
- Consistent in thoughts, words, and actions
- Confident enough to be vulnerable
- Able to put a positive twist on difficulties

Perceptions are critical. Great communicators understand that perceptions are powerful, and they use this knowledge to their advantage. If you perceive yourself in a positive fashion, you will project that way, and others will react to you the same way. If you project a negative attitude, they'll react to you that way, too.

How do you create the right perceptions? Whenever you go into a meeting, see yourself as being tops in your field — no matter what that field is. If you're a singer, see yourself as singing like Kiri Te Kanawa or Luciano Pavarotti. If you're a painter, see yourself as Georgia O'Keeffe or Pablo Picasso. See the world in line wanting to buy your paintings. If you're a salesperson, think you're selling three times quota and you have job offers from all over. If you get the feeling of being good, you'll start to react that way — not aggressive, but confident, in focus, and aligned.

Your goal is to connect with your partner so the two of you can better understand each other. The time to evaluate comes later. Evaluate what's said, not the person saying it. Your partner deserves your respect, even if you disagree with his or her ideas. To connect, you must give your partner the benefit of the doubt.

ATTITUDE RULES

Aptitude is your inherent ability to do something if you're trained. Skill results from training and practice. *Attitude* is the desire to do it. When your attitude is poor, no amount of skill or aptitude can help. Attitude can and will make the difference. Effective communicators are optimistic and confident they can't fail.

— **Robert**

AUDITORY WORDS

Short words are best and the old words, when short, are best of all.
— WINSTON CHURCHILL

Different types of people express themselves in, and respond to, different types of words, depending on the way they perceive the world around them (see *Sensory Words*). Auditory people relate to the world through their ears. You can recognize them by their use of words such as the following, and you should use words like these to get your ideas across to them.

Accent	Discuss	Listen
Ask	Earful	Loud and clear
Brilliant	Echo	Manner of speaking
Buzz	Hazy	Monotonous
Call on	Heard	On the same wavelength
Call out	Heard voices	Outspoken
Clang	I hear you	Rap session
Clarify	Idle talk	Recite
Clear as a bell	Inspect	Rhythm

Ring	Sounds good to me	Tongue-tied
Ringing sound	Sounds like	Turns a deaf ear
Rings a bell	Talk to you later	Unheard of
Say	To tell the truth	Voiced an opinion
So to speak	Tone	Whine

WHAT'S IMPORTANT WHEN WE COMMUNICATE?

We have difficulty communicating because we don't listen to what's important and often don't say what's necessary.

Think about someone you know very well. If you asked her, "Do you understand what I said?" in which way would she reply?

— "I see what you mean. It looks easy."
— "I've got a good grasp of the details. Let's get going." Or,
— "I hear you, sounds good."

If this person would respond the last way, then her response is auditory. By choosing auditory words for auditory people, you help them more readily interpret what you're saying.

Your response might be, "Well if it *sounds* good, let's stop *talking* and start doing."

USE THE RIGHT SENSE WHEN COMMUNICATING

"You aren't *listening* to me!" exclaimed my friend. The customer service rep said, "What I *heard* you say was . . . " and then asked if that *sounded* right. My friend said yes. She then said, "Let me *tell you* what I can do to help." The service rep communicated clearly using auditory words. My friend understood and the problem was corrected.

— Robert

BEHAVIORAL LANGUAGE

The most you can hope for is to have the other person listen, understand, and consider the benefits of your proposal. Deliver your message in their language and you will accomplish just that.
— PETER

We all have certain specific behavioral tendencies. That's not to say we're pigeonholed into being one thing or another. We are not locked into these tendencies — but more times than not, we tend to behave the same way again and again. Why? By default, we return to what we feel is safe and comfortable.

Often we ask ourselves, "Why did he say that?" "Why did he do that?" or "Who does he think he is?" These questions might be rephrased as, "Why did you say that?" "Why did you do that?" and "Who do you think you are?" Each of us is different. Fortunately we are *predictably* different and our differences make us simultaneously attractive and frustrating to others.

The secret of persuasion is to understand yourself and others. Then you can adapt effectively to the needs of the person and the situation. Information is power, but it's only powerful if you know how to obtain and use it.

David Golman, author of *Emotional Intelligence,* defined "EQ" as an ability to understand one's own feelings and to express empathy for the feelings of others. His studies showed that *EQ is four times more likely than IQ to indicate your level of success.* According to Golman, the communication skills responsible for EQ are

— Empathy
— Graciousness
— The ability to read others

Since ancient times, humankind has attempted to read others and explain the reason for their differences. Credible personality models have been traced as far back as the writings of Hippocrates, Aristotle, and Galen. For a comparison of the better-known personality profiles, see *Differences.*

The ability to influence others is dependent on the degree of willingness you and your partner wish to exercise in being cooperative and getting along. The greater your ability to adapt to your partner's behavior and to communicate in his language, the more receptive he will be to you and the greater your chance of success will be.

The key to influencing others lies in your ability to present your needs in terms of meeting *their* needs, and in wording your proposal in a way that is most receptive and understandable to *them.* In short, we want benefits spelled out for us in our own language. We want these benefits presented in a way that we can understand, so that we can put them to good use.

If you want to influence someone, *you* have to do the work of delivering your message in the receiver's behavioral language. *You* must design your presentations to meet his needs so he can immediately see the benefits.

To sum up:

— You have a preferred behavioral pattern
— You also have the ability to modify it to suit the situation and environment

— This ability makes you uniquely gifted and tremendously effective as a communicator

LANGUAGE BARRIERS EXIST —
EVEN IN THE SAME LANGUAGE

A few years ago, the British division of the McDonald's hamburger chain suffered a serious public relations blow. Try as they might to dispel them, rumors persisted that the company supported the Irish Republican Army.

After spending a lot of time and money investigating, McDonald's finally solved the mystery. The rumor had begun when a CNN broadcast was carried in England. It reported that McDonald's senior management encouraged its employees to invest in IRAs. In the U.S., IRA means "Individual Retirement Account."

In Britain, of course, IRA stands for "Irish Republican Army." A simple acronym can mean drastically different things to different people. You may be sending out negative signals without even knowing it!

— **Robert**

BODY CLUES

Even the smallest actions become gestures, and gestures transmit messages.
— Desmond Morris

You can use body clues to predict a whole range of actions. Body movements indicate things about another person that may have great importance for creating communication — or give you reasons to avoid it. Here are a few easy-to-spot characteristics that can help you determine whether it's wise to continue your present course of action.

1. READINESS AND ENTHUSIASM

When people are ready to take action, they'll often sit forward in their seats or stand with their hands on their hips. They are anxious to get going. They will stand or sit in an erect position. They are alert, with wide, bright eyes. Their body motions are alive and animated. Their words can't keep up with their hands. When you see these signs, get going — because they're ready!

2. FRUSTRATION

Most of us are familiar with these signs. How many times a day do you see some of these gestures: hand-wringing, running fingers through hair, clenching hands or jaw, an exasperated sigh, or tension in the small muscles of the face? If you see these signs in others, retreat before approaching with any request!

3. SUPERIORITY

People who feel superior to you often appear relaxed, with their hands clasped behind their heads or backs. The chin and head is often held high. They may lean back in their chairs, or lean their bodies against a wall, table, or desk. When someone behaves this way it's important for you to control your emotions, apply your communication skills, and focus on the issues at hand.

4. BOREDOM

Bored people tap their fingers or feet. They're often preoccupied with personal grooming or with other insignificant details, such as sharpening a pencil. They will also point their bodies to the door, and often check their watches. Often, asking a question or stating your observation of their behaviors will involve them in the conversation.

5. NERVOUSNESS

Nervous people cover their mouths when they speak. Their voices are often high, and may even break. Their speech is hesitant, and they use "ums" and "ahs" incessantly. They may clear their throats and wring their hands while looking down at their shoes. You may also see their facial muscles twitching as they shift back and forth on their feet. It's important for you to create a safe environment for them to speak, to maintain rapport, and to be patient and encouraging.

BODY LANGUAGE TELLS A TALE

I remember staying out overnight once as a teenager. When I came home, I told my mother that I had stayed with a friend. And I had stayed with a friend — a young female friend. I looked my mother in the eye and told her that I had stayed with a friend. She knew I wasn't talking about a male friend. I will never know to this day how she recognized that white lie, but I felt as if my nose had grown an inch.

— **Peter**

BODY LANGUAGE

Watch for the man whose stomach doesn't move when he laughs.

— CHINESE PROVERB

"A hint taken, a look understood, conveys the gist of long and delicate explanation . . . In the closest of all relations — that of a love well-founded and equally shared — speech is half discarded." So says the novelist Robert Louis Stevenson. He is emphasizing that we need to hear with our eyes, not just with our ears. Body language is *the major* key to understanding, and while it's important to observe it in others, these same signs transmit messages about us.

One caution — several supportive gestures are a more reliable indicator than a single gesture.

EYES

The eyes, according to Leonardo da Vinci, are the "mirror to the soul."

— Confident eye contact shows trustworthiness and truthfulness.
— Shifty eyes indicate aloofness and distrust.

— In North America, two to six seconds is considered normal contact (with increasing cultural diversity, we need to become more comfortable with more and less eye contact).

— If someone won't maintain eye contact it may mean they are uncomfortable with either you or the topic.

— Intent staring is considered aggressive.

— Maintaining eye contact marks us as confident, credible, and connected.

— Related indicators include raising the eyebrows in disbelief, scrunching the face (as in frowning), and winking.

POSTURE

Posture both reflects and affects how we feel.

— Sloppy posture occurs when we're too loose.

— If we're too stiff, we appear tense and stressed.

— Crossed legs may signal disagreement and self-protection.

— When we're withdrawn and holding our heads down, we appear weak, indecisive, and lacking in confidence.

— With a confident posture, our heads are up and we're sitting and standing erect.

— Develop a confident, brisk walk, with freely swinging arms. A self-assured person moves with purpose.

HANDS AND ARMS

Our hands and arms say a lot about us. Gestures are sometimes deliberate, but most often they occur unconsciously and naturally. If we're stuck for words, our gestures become more animated, as if to replace missing words and express things that words seem incapable of expressing.

— Arms across the chest indicate that we're protecting ourselves, or we're cold.

— Open hands and arms, especially extended, indicate openness and welcome.

— Hands with palms up in front of the body at chest height indicate importance.

— The same gesture to the sides of the chest signals frustration or helplessness.

— A pointing finger or a hand waving above the shoulders emphasizes a point.

— Two hands above the head signals victory.

— Hands to the mouth might indicate that we're hiding something.

— Fidgeting with our hands? We might be sending the message that we're nervous.

— Hands clasped behind the lower back may indicate security and confidence.

— Hands in front of the groin area could be defensive or protective.

— Shrugging our shoulders may be interpreted as not caring about the meaning of the message being sent.

— Gestures around the face are considered defensive, much like a boxer with hands raised to ward off blows.

— Tightly clenched hands indicate anger or tension.

— Rubbing the ear might be a sign of doubt.

— Rubbing the back of the neck could indicate frustration.

— Resting hands on the chin and allowing eyelids to droop indicates boredom or tiredness.

— Stroking the chin indicates contemplation or thought.

— Sitting back in a relaxed position with fingers steepled indicates self-assurance.

HANDSHAKES

What about those handshakes? How we shake hands is culturally determined, yet — whether right or wrong — perceptions about us are determined by how we shake hands.

— Is it loose and wimpy or tight and aggressive?

— In North America, a handshake should be web-to-web (with the base of your thumb to theirs), confident, and firm. Typically, it might take about three seconds, include three to five good pumps, and include good eye contact.

— Adapt your handshake to that of the other person. Allow him or her to guide how firmly and how long it takes.

WATCH HOW OTHERS USE BODY LANGUAGE

Whenever I sit in any airport, railway station, or hotel lobby, I watch people using the telephone. When people make a call, you can tell if they're speaking to a loved one (they hold the phone very close), to a boss (they'll sit up straight), or to a person of real authority (they'll often hold the phone away from themselves). If they use a cell phone to have a very personal conversation, they often walk into a corner to be more private.

To become aware of body language, observe other people. Lovers, fighters — all these people are wonderful to observe, and it's much better to observe these situations than to be in them!

Quickly now: when you interlock your fingers, which thumb is uppermost? Try to reverse their positions consciously. Your hand posture will feel strange and awkward. That's how unconscious and telling body language is.

— Peter

BOSSES

Regardless of what you do, you only have one job — to get your boss promoted. If you focus on that, you're doing everything in your job that you need to do.
— ROBERT

We all answer to someone. Bosses come in all shapes and sizes and have many different styles, yet they speak the same language — the bottom line. How you communicate with your boss will have an impact on your performance evaluation, your raise, and your career.

Here are some tips on communicating with your boss:

- Propose, don't impose, solutions to problems
- Share all the information — good and bad
- Don't take the boss's decisions personally
- Clarify resources, levels of authority, responsibilities, reporting schedules, desired outcomes, and deadlines
- Ask for feedback

A BOSS COULD BE YOU

You will meet people who are scared of the boss, no matter who the boss is. People of power inspire fear and awe. But the more you get in touch with your own self, you will see that although you're not better than others, you are also not less than others. I didn't learn this in a philosophy class. I discovered it out of my life's experiences. I thought I was better than certain groups of people, and that meant, of course, that I was inferior to other groups — especially bosses. Bosses are simply people who have been "loaned" some authority. Once you come to terms with yourself, you will begin to level your playing field — with both bosses and subordinates.

— **Peter**

BREATHING

Breathing is important. Don't ever try to stop or neglect it for too long.
— PETER

Generally speaking, our feelings are reflected by our rate of breathing and general physiology. If we're nervous, startled, or excited, we breathe rapidly and shallowly. If we're relaxed, comfortable, or contemplative, we breathe more deeply. This is an important factor in understanding other people. By adopting their breathing rates and postures, you will begin to feel similar feelings and better understand what they're thinking.

Sometimes it's difficult to determine what people's breathing rates are. Watch the edges of their shoulders. See how they move against the background and then try to match it. In addition, adopt their general body position to get fully into their state of mind.

But be careful. If their breathing rate is considerably different from yours, the matching can be exhausting for you to maintain. Don't do it for too long. In any case, the objective is to match them, not slavishly copy them. In fact, once you establish contact and develop understanding for how they are feeling, you may begin to breathe and speak at your normal rate.

A DEMONSTRATION PROVES THE POINT

I've seen this demonstrated time and again in front of live audiences. Two people who are unknown to each other are asked to come to the front of the room. One is asked to recall an experience from his past and relive it as completely as possible in his mind. The other person is simply asked to observe and match the first person's rate of breathing and body position.

After about five minutes, the person who has copied the body position and breathing rate of the first person is asked what she is feeling. Invariably, both people's feelings are similar.

Want to increase your ability to empathize? Adopt a similar body position and breathing rate to your partner's — unbelievable, but true.

— **Robert**

BROKEN RECORD

You hate to do it, but sometimes you need to repeat yourself ten times. The trick is to repeat yourself with a smile.
— PETER

Broken records don't move forward. Some of us remember those vinyl records from long, long ago. The needle would get stuck and the same part of the music would play over and over again. Sometimes people get stuck and try to sidetrack you or change the topic. They will attempt to go over, under, or around you. Use the broken record to stick to the topic, to get a response to a question, or to simply say "no."

Here's how you do it:

— Focus on and state what you want
— Acknowledge what they've said if they sidetrack you
— Repeat what you said

This powerful technique is simple and effective — yet it's not easy in practice.

IT'S BEYOND MY CONTROL

A woman who worked for a state welfare organization once confided that many recipients who were eligible for benefits didn't receive them because they were negligent in filling out their forms on time. She felt bad about this but was unable to do anything about it. The recipients would curse at her, blame her, and accuse her of all sorts of things. I explained how the broken record technique could help her.

- State the conditions for getting the benefits when they scream, "You don't care what happens to me!"

- Acknowledge what they said and repeat the conditions. "I do care, and that's why I wish you'd filled out the forms on time."

- When they counter with, "My children will be out on the street," acknowledge by saying, "I wish you had filled the forms out in time to prevent any problems this will cause you."

- Continue in this fashion until they realize you aren't going to give in.

— **Robert**

BULLDOZERS

The bigger they are, the harder they fall.
— COMMON PROVERB

We've all met difficult characters. They can't be avoided, so we have to deal with them. Here are some suggestions on dealing with one of the better-known types — the Bulldozer.

With Bulldozers, it's their way or the highway. Bulldozers aren't necessarily hostile, but they are fast-acting, decisive, and motivated to get results. When you deal with Bulldozers, you're either going to help them or get in their way.

Here are some tips on how to handle Bulldozers:

— Remain calm, hold eye contact, and breathe
— Hear them out, then reflect their main concerns
— Focus on the bottom line — be brief
— Offer options — they're decisive
— Avoid a battle, because they won't back down
— If possible, allow them the last word

MY FATHER, THE BULLDOZER

People will judge you by your actions. You may have a heart of gold — but so does a hard-boiled egg.

I had a hard time understanding my father, who was very direct and to the point. Rarely did he mince words. He usually wouldn't ask you to do something — he would tell you. If I confronted him about his manner or his "way," he wouldn't back down. In fact, he became more determined to have it done his way — the only way, in his mind. Even when he meant well, and he often did, he had no time for niceties or discussion.

When you're having a conversation with a Bulldozer, focus on the issue, be brief, and don't be intimidated. A Bulldozer is who he is — focused on the issue, direct, and intimidating.

— **Robert**

CHECKING IT OUT

The only person who behaves sensibly is my tailor. He takes new measurements every time he sees me. Everyone else uses their old measurements.
— GEORGE BERNARD SHAW

We've all had them . . . those embarrassing moments when we enter a promising conversation, and somehow one of our pet peeves emerges. Before you can button your lip, you're saying something like, "I hate teachers" (or lawyers, government employees, politicians, whatever — apply the necessary vocation — use only one!).

You can still ride your hobby horse (if it seems necessary), but before you do, it makes a great deal of sense to start your conversation by asking your partner what he or she does. Questions like " . . . and you work with what company?" or "What is your job?" or, more bluntly, "What do you do for a living?" not only indicate interest in your partner, but they will stop you from making rash statements. If you don't and he or she replies, "Too bad. *I'm* a (teacher, lawyer, etc.) . . . ," where do you go from there?

Use questions to check your ground. There is a lot of ground to cover. Facing an individual for the first time, or facing a committee whose members you don't know, are similar experiences. You need to ask questions to get to know the "lay of the land." Just like a military scout, you need to listen, observe, and then start questioning the rules that underlie a conversation just as soon as introductions are made. Here are a few things you might want to check out.

QUESTION HIDDEN AGENDAS

If you hear any of these comments, be careful! They may be disguising the speaker's hidden agenda, and should raise the hairs on the back of your neck.

- — Everybody's doing it.
- — Let me tell you what is really happening!
- — I'm your friend. Would I lie to you?
- — It's exactly the same as before. You don't have to check it.
- — It's okay. Trust me.
- — We're alone in this. We have to stick together.

Also listen for any one-sided, biased evidence or any emotional hot button your partner or colleague tries to push.

QUESTION ASSUMPTIONS — THEIRS AND YOURS

Assumptions must be shared for effective communication. If you're having trouble understanding each other, check out both sets of assumptions. Question the reason behind your areas of disagreement to find your underlying differences.

For instance: You may reach an impasse when it comes time to sign on the dotted line. Your partner is hesitating. You become confused because your partner seemed excited by the proposal and was fully involved in the presentation. State what you observed: "I'm confused because you seemed to be interested in the proposal and now you're reluctant to proceed. Why is that?"

You may discover some underlying assumption you were originally unaware of. Maybe your partner likes the proposal, but feels product reliability isn't good. Whatever the reason, now is the time to find out.

QUESTION THINGS YOU DON'T UNDERSTAND

Clarify misunderstandings and confusion immediately. Take the responsibility to understand your partner and his message. Show your partner that you're paying attention and you want to understand what is being said.

QUESTION HOW IT IS SAID

How something is said is often more important than what is said. Many people simply don't realize *how* they are saying something. If you sense something that bothers you in the way something is said, address it immediately.

For instance: In the middle of helping someone, you hear agitation or frustration in the person's tone of voice. Be specific and take ownership of how you feel about it. You might say, "I sense you're frustrated. Is that true?" Don't criticize. Focus on the message you are getting and see if you can straighten it out.

QUESTION NON-SPECIFIC WORDS

If someone says, "He went to the store," ask who he is. If your partner says, "They took it with them," ask specifically who *they* are and what *it* was they took. Don't make assumptions about non-specific words.

Think like a detective. You come home and find your house broken into and some of your possessions stolen. You see your neighbors next door and immediately ask them if they saw or heard anything. They tell you that, at about 3 p.m., they saw a man and woman get into a car and drive away. You immediately want to know what kind of car they had and which direction they went in. Can they give you a description of the man and woman? Did they recognize the pair? Non-specific information isn't going to help you or the police.

QUESTION DELETIONS AND DISTORTIONS

Perhaps something appears wrong, missing, or avoided in your conversation. Try to determine what appears to be deleted or exaggerated.

For instance: A car salesman tells you that the engine of the car you're interested in gets more than 185 miles to the gallon. That seems exaggerated, even unbelievable. Ask for proof to confirm the fact.

Another example: You're mediating a conflict between two co-workers. As you question them, seeking clues to help them resolve the conflict, you notice that while giving you their versions of the conflict, they are each leaving out important details. Question those deletions. You need complete information to help them.

QUESTION ABSOLUTES

Absolute words become imperatives — they dictate that one should do or think about something in one way only. They limit your thinking, actions, and creativity. Question them. Look for signposts such as "would," "should," "must," "can't," "ought to," and "may not."

But questioning your partner about such words requires great sensitivity, because the speaker often feels as though his or her values are being questioned and judged. Soften the questioning by asking, "I wonder what you mean when you say . . . ?" Or ask, "I'm confused. Why *should* I? I'm puzzled. Why *can't* I?" Or consider asking, "What would happen if I did or didn't?"

A good example: Your boss says you can't do what you are planning and stops you from doing something you wanted to try. Ask, "I'm not sure I understand. Why can't I do that? What would happen if I did?"

QUESTION GENERALIZATIONS

"Never," "always," "every," and "everybody" are all generalizations. They're all fair game to explore.

For example: Your teenage son wants to stay out late. His argument is that *everyone* else can. Do you know one other teen who can't stay out late? If you do, his argument (if not necessarily his action) is shot down. The point is that if an exception exists, the whole assumption, or generalization, is untrue. The exception to this is when the generalization is shared and your partner agrees to accept it "for argument's sake."

QUESTION COMPARISONS

Comparisons such as "better," "worse," "easier," and such are also open to question. Better than what? Worse than whom? Easier than what, specifically?

Comparisons with others are usually unjustified. The only true comparison should be with yourself, or against your expected standards of performance. Focus on specific performance improvements or deteriorations.

For example: Your boss tells you that a particular task is easy. You might want to ask her, "Easier than what?" Because she finds it easy is irrelevant. Her skill set is likely different than yours. Maybe it wasn't so easy the first time she tried it. Question comparisons. You be the judge of how easy it is.

STRANGE QUESTIONS SAY A LOT

I first met Joe in our freshman year of university. Later, he and I became roommates. One Sunday evening, Joe asked me, "Do you love your parents?" I thought this a strange question. First, guys don't talk this way to other guys — at least 19-year-old guys don't. Second, I wasn't sure how to respond, so I tried to answer the question as best I could.

Later in life, I came to realize that when someone asks a question out of the blue, he or she usually wants to tell you something. I would have done better if I had ignored the *content* of Joe's question and checked out the *intent*. Whenever you're in doubt, ask a question and check it out.

— **Robert**

CLOSED QUESTIONS

There are no wrong answers, only unasked questions.
— ROBERT

When you deliver your question, the listener goes within to retrieve and interpret feelings and ideas. It takes time to access the information before the listener can externalize answers. As the person asking the question, you need to verify and acknowledge your understanding, and continue to go deeper into the questioning cycle until you complete the loop.

The most important part of any question is the response it evokes, and you should distinguish clearly between two different types or classes of questions: closed questions and open questions.

Closed questions are used to gather specific or factual information. They're the most commonly used type of questions, and will generally get you only a "yes" or "no" response. A typical closed question might be "What day is it?" or "Do you want this?" The questions are simple, straightforward, and direct.

Closed questions are easy to answer, and are often used to direct a conversation. They push you to take a position or be committed to a cause.

Because they're used to gather information, they can also be used to determine accuracy. Closed questions can also be used to influence a person's response.

The *tag-on question* is a variation of the closed question. This kind of question is used to invite agreement or disagreement. Take the question "Dale, you think this is a good offer, don't you?" as an example. The question begs the answer "yes" or "no." Tag-on questions are effective but can be maddening, especially if they are overused. They can occur at the beginning, middle, or end of a statement.

If you want specific facts, if you want to understand each other, or if you want to control the direction of a conversation, ask closed questions.

BEING COURTEOUS WITH CLOSED QUESTIONS

It's far better to probe for conclusions than to jump to them. A simple closed question can gather facts, gain commitment, and tell your partner what you're about to discuss. I learned this by trial and error.

I used to drop by the offices of my colleagues unannounced and then come right to the point — my point. While my partner often seemed attentive, I noticed that many times that person appeared preoccupied or tried to multi-task by listening to me while continuing to do something else.

In order to get this person's full attention, I adopted the habit of asking a closed question: "Is this a good time to discuss . . . ?" If the answer was "yes," I would proceed. If it was "no," I would establish a better time to return.

I discovered that this person became more cooperative when I used this method. By the way, it's also more courteous.

— Robert

| COLLABORATION

Collaboration allows you to discover things together with someone else that you might not ever have discovered alone.
— PETER

Collaboration is characterized by the sum of the parts being greater than the whole. Collaboration is a joint effort by two or more people in which individual interests are subordinated to group unity and coordinated effort. The end result is typically different than what either party might have done individually — and it's often superior.

Groupthink is a condition that occurs in teams when they know each other too well. They no longer challenge each other or question ideas. They act and think as a single unit. At first glance, this might seem to be the ideal state. However, the problem with this condition is insufficient challenge and variety.

The best ideas require alternatives, challenges to the accepted norms, and diversity. When you're working as part of a group, welcome differences of all kinds. In fact, encourage them. Each person must bring a new perspective to the table. This often creates conflict, but conflict can be good if it stimulates thought, focuses on the issues, and challenges the dreaded "We've always done it this way" thinking.

ONE STEP BETTER — OR MORE

The best question I have ever asked is, "What one thing would you suggest?"

Often, when asked for input, others won't comment for fear of hurting your feelings.

I remember asking someone to comment on my proposal — a proposal that I didn't particularly like. The woman replied that it was good. Rather than challenge her reply, I asked her, "What one thing would you suggest to improve it?" She suggested three things and we came up with a much better proposal.

Is there someone who sees things differently than you do? Ask her for one thing. You'll get more than you bargained for.

— **Robert**

| COMFORT ZONE

Each of us has an instinctive barrier to proximity.
The distance between aggressive and passive can be a
matter of inches.
— ROBERT

When is too close close enough? We all have a "comfort zone." The distance between polite and rude varies from culture to culture. In North America, however, the following general rules apply:

— The intimate comfort zone reserved for lovers and close family is from zero to eighteen inches
— For friends and acquaintances, the comfort zone is between eighteen inches and four feet
— Beyond four feet is reserved for very important dignitaries or formal presentations

Be aware that cultural differences exist. Know your communication partner's comfort zone. If you ignore it, you will have trouble connecting. What's more, you'll be perceived as aggressive if you stand too close and passive if you stand too far away. Follow your partner's lead.

WATCH PEOPLE AT A PARTY

At parties, I've noticed that the comfort zone tends to change with the consumption of a little alcohol. Inhibitions are lessened, voices tend to get louder, people giggle more. When people are comfortable and having a good time, they tend to be freer and bend the comfort zone rules a lot more. The next time you're at a party, watch how people's comfort zones change.

— **Peter**

| COMPLAINERS

He reminds me of the man who murdered both his parents, and then when the sentence was about to be pronounced, pleaded for mercy on the grounds that he was an orphan.
— ABRAHAM LINCOLN

We've all met difficult characters. They can't be avoided, so we have to deal with them. Here are some suggestions on dealing with one of the better-known types — the Complainer.

"There is one topic peremptorily forbidden to all well bred, to all rational mortals, namely, their distempers. If you have not slept, or if you have slept, or if you have headache, or sciatica, or leprosy, or thunderstroke, I beseech you, by all angels, to hold your peace, and not pollute the morning." So said Ralph Waldo Emerson, and he was reflecting on what is actually a learned behavior. Complainers and whiners have learned that you'll take care of them if they whine.

Here are some tips on how to deal with Complainers:

— Listen without agreeing.
— Help them get to the point.
— Help them be specific, not general.
— Summarize what they've said.

— Ask for solutions — insist that they provide options. Explain what you can do and what you can't do, then let them choose from your list of can-do's.

— Set boundaries by showing them the consequences of their complaining.

EXAGGERATION TRUMPS EVERY TIME

If you meet two people complaining about something and a third one joins them, that person's aim is to trump the first two. When Complainers get together, some amusing things can happen. I remember so well the case of an author dealing with an art director and an artist. The art director complained he was paid so little he had holes in his pockets, and pulled out a pants pocket to prove it. The artist said he was paid so little he had holes in his shoes, and showed the holes. The author said, "That's nothing." He pulled out his credit card and the numbers were worn off. Then he added, "And I have holes in my pockets *and* holes in my shoes, too."

— **Robert**

| CONNECTING

Connecting is a lot like dancing: You need the right partner, someone needs to lead, and you need to establish a rhythm.
— ROBERT

We do things for our own reasons, not someone else's. That's why you need to position what you want to correspond with what your partner wants. It puts you and your partner on the same wavelength. *People don't care how much you know until they know how much you care.* Connecting demonstrates how much you care.

Connecting won't ensure you will like each other. In fact, liking isn't important for connection. Effective communication is possible between two individuals who dislike each other personally, provided they focus on the outcome and not on each other.

Connection leads to better understanding because it creates

— Harmony
— Trust
— Believability

Connection happens on many levels. Remember the last time you fell in love with a place, a color, a painting, a piece of music, or a book? You became connected with it. These inanimate things have the power to move you. It's the same way with interpersonal connection, only with a more powerful result, because you get the chance to move the other person.

Connection allows you to understand and be understood. But how do you know if you're connected? Instinct tells you.

Remember a time when your partner said something that upset you. Maybe it was the words that were said. Maybe it was the way they were said. Maybe it was something in your partner's body language that caused a sudden feeling of tension. That was a message from your subconscious reminding you that connection is a function of trust.

If you feel comfortable, chances are the other person feels the same. If you feel uneasy or uncomfortable, if your conversation feels unnatural, or if you're struggling to get along, you're not connected. Your partner probably feels the same.

Many of the techniques we use for connection involve copying our partner's behavior and actions. Do this subtly and without exaggeration. Less is always more. Just be aware of differences and stay flexible. We call the techniques *focus, match,* and *ignore.*

- *Focus* on your partner's emotional and mental state
- *Match* virtually anything you notice about your partner's words, voice, and body language
- *Ignore* everything that annoys and distracts you

The true test of connection: Can you assume the conversational lead and have your partner follow your argument, body position, or action? If not, then follow their lead until you can.

TRUST IS THE KEY

When you fell in love with your spouse, you were connected with all your senses. Unfortunately, connections may not last forever, even when you are married! Lasting connections must be built on trust.

Communication connections must be established and re-established each time you communicate. They must also be maintained throughout any conversation — and any relationship.

— Peter

CRITICISM

Think of criticism as feedback — feedback about how your partner perceives your actions.
— ROBERT

Sometimes criticism is deserved; sometimes it's not. You won't know until you've heard and understood the criticism. If you cut the person off, you'll end the feedback or damage the relationship.

HOW TO RECEIVE CRITICISM

Under ideal conditions

— *Listen*
— Be receptive and open-minded
— Summarize for understanding
— Suspend your judgment and don't be defensive
— Thank the person for offering you the feedback

If you decide to do something about the criticism you've received, get feedback from the person about how well you're doing.

In reality

— Even when you're ready for it, once in a while criticism is difficult to take. Consider the source and the level of his or her expertise.

— No matter how stable, sensible, and receptive you are, sometimes the criticism hits a nerve and you mentally wish the person laying it on you would vanish into thin air. Focus on the truth in this statement and ignore the rest.

— Don't worry about it, it's normal — froth at the mouth a bit in private, then forget it.

IN EVERY GROUP OF 30 THERE'S AT LEAST ONE CRITIC

I used to teach public speaking at Ryerson Polytechnic University in Toronto. During one session, I remember explaining how to deal with criticism as laid out above. At the end of the class, one of my students (who had never been particularly attentive) asked me what credentials I had to teach a course on public speaking at such a well-known Canadian university. I could feel the hairs rise on the back of my neck, and I just wanted to smack the guy. What made me even madder was that I had just finished explaining how dealing with criticism is easy.

There's no doubt that when you are hit unexpectedly, or in a vulnerable area, criticism still stings, and it's almost impossible not to take it personally. When it hurts, the impulse (no matter how well-controlled you are) is to hurt back.

— **Peter**

CRYING

Crying is a natural way of expressing many different emotions — we cry for both joy and sorrow. But what do we do if it's unexpected, if it's happening to us, or if it's happening to someone we're communicating with? Follow these steps.

If someone else starts to cry

- Offer a tissue
- Call a "time-out"
- Say to yourself, "Nonetheless . . . " and carry on if you must

If you feel like you're going to start to cry

- Pretend to sneeze and ask for a tissue
- Blame your allergies
- Ask for a glass of water
- Fake dropping a contact lens or something

— Excuse yourself temporarily

— Admit this is very important to you and continue

CRYING — WHAT A RELIEF!

If you watch the Olympics on television, you'll notice that it's usually the winners who cry — whether this is from relief or joy scarcely matters. It's the overwhelming emotional response to winning that brings it on. But shouldn't the losers be the ones to cry?

— Peter

*D*IFFERENCES

You attract individuals who are like you.
— PETER

O ur external behavior — behavior that is obvious to those around us — is only the tip of the iceberg. Below the surface, submerged in the hidden depths, lie our feelings, attitudes, beliefs, values, inherent personality, and personal experiences.

Add to the above differences of gender, generation, education, and culture, as well as differences of communication style, and it's easy to understand why others behave so differently and unexpectedly. The more aware we are of these differences, the better prepared we are to communicate accurately and easily.

Since the days of Hippocrates, Aristotle, and Galen, attempts have been made to read others and to classify behavioral patterns. Today, most models describe personality types rather than behavioral differences. But as leaders and communicators, we aren't interested in a person's personality or psychological type. While it may be interesting, this is really the concern of qualified psychologists.

What we are interested in is a person's *behavior.* We shouldn't pigeon-hole a person by a specific behavior pattern. It's better to remain open and flexible and try to understand how that person is changing from moment to moment.

It pays to understand, nevertheless, that there are four broad behavioral styles (more, according to some authorities) that allow us to determine the way a person is behaving at the moment. These styles also give us the ability to respond appropriately to their actions.

While behavioral types are identifiable, there is no right or wrong pattern. Tremendous overlap exists between the four identifiable types. Each of us uses these four patterns to varying degrees at different times. Each of us also has the flexibility to change our behavioral responses under stress, when things are going well, and in other situations.

Each one of us does, however, have a preferred behavioral pattern with specific backup patterns. Knowing someone else's preferred behavioral pattern permits you to anticipate and prepare your message in a way that he or she will understand. When the message is understood, the receiver will be more apt to receive the message positively.

In order to influence others, we must be able to react and change our own behavior according to how the other person is behaving. The fact remains, however, that we are most effective as communicators when we interact with people who are similar to us. The problem arises when the listener is different from us, and that's where understanding differences can help.

We all believe two things:

— We are right about how we see, think, and act — so if you don't agree with us, you must be wrong.
— Other people see life the same way we do — or at least they should!

The bottom line is that each personality type has different needs, values, motivations, and levels of assertiveness and responsiveness. We name the four types as follows:

1. The Expressive: Get attention. *Symbol:* Peacock (see *The Expressive*)
2. The Driver: Get it done. *Symbol:* Eagle (see *The Driver*)
3. The Amiable: Get along. *Symbol:* Dove (see *The Amiable*)
4. The Analytical: Get it right. *Symbol:* Owl (see *The Analytical*)

Find ways of understanding and dealing with these different behavioral types in the sections dealing with each of them.

Remember, there is no right or wrong behavior. Each of us can demonstrate any one of these behaviors. Persuading others depends on two things: being able to identify the behavior, and responding appropriately to it.

Often in seminars I'll group the Analyticals, Drivers, Amiables, and Expressives into separate groups and give them five minutes to plan their ideal vacations.

— The Analyticals typically plan a trip well into the future. They know the date, the flight, the hotels, and so on. They know exactly when and where they are going — with complete daily agendas for the trip. So organized!

— The Drivers argue. They don't have time to go on a trip. There is too much to do. They argue about when they should go on a trip. They have a hard time coming to terms, because each of them wants to be in control.

— The Amiables can't decide. They attempt to reach a consensus and are very sensitive to upsetting someone's feelings. They are very supportive and accommodating. Usually time runs out and the details of their trip are, at best, sketchy.

— The Expressives are loud and boisterous. They're ready to go now with what they're wearing. "Let's find a sell-off! Let's go last minute! We can buy what we need when we get there." You can tell the party has already started!

The objective here is not to paint a complete portrait of each of these behavioral types, or even to help you to take a personality analysis to identify your own dominant behavior pattern. It is, rather, to help you understand how to *communicate* with each type.

A detailed explanation of personality analysis is found in *Leadership from Within* by Peter Urs Bender, in the section "Understanding Your Personality Type" (pp. 59–83). The test itself is included in the Appendix of *Leadership from Within* (pp. 234–36). Or you can visit the web site www.SecretsofFacetoFaceCommunication.com and take the test there.

LEARNING TO LIVE WITH DIFFERENCES

I used to argue over details with Lori, a co-worker of mine some years ago. She needed them and they slowed me down. "Jump in and learn by doing" was my motto — one that I considered to be much more spontaneous than her cautious approach.

Where I felt bogged down by too many details, Lori wanted to know what, where, why, when, who, and how. Obviously, we were both right. Facts are important, but relying on them too much can be confining.

People who are different from us challenge our weaknesses, provide diversity in our thinking, and cause us to grow. If only I had appreciated that small gem earlier in my life.

Remember: People are *different,* not *difficult.*

— Robert

DISTRACTIONS

It's not hocus-pocus, it's focus-focus!
— ROBERT

The *HEART* approach to active listening includes "H" for *Hush,* the need for freedom from disturbance. It is important to have as little distraction as possible in order for successful communication to take place.

Disturbances can be both internal and external. Internal disturbances include

- Perceptions
- Experiences
- Emotions
- Your own thoughts
- Emotional prejudices
- Your own physical health
- Poor communication skills

External disturbances include

— Things you're doing
— Things your partner is doing
— What's going on around you

When internal disturbances occur, try to refocus on your goal. Ask "What's my purpose for talking to this person?" If, on the other hand, your partner tunes out or loses track, ask a question to help refocus his or her thinking. One way to quiet your mind is to be prepared. Successful communicators are well-informed. Be as prepared as possible prior to important meetings.

Stop talking. Concentrate 100 percent on your partner and his or her message. This doesn't mean that you should stop asking questions or stop encouraging your partner with gestures and comments such as "Tell me more." It does mean that you should stop interrupting. Use comments or questions to indicate that you are focusing on your partner's message — nothing more, nothing less.

Try to change external distractions. Distractions can be maddening when you're trying to achieve connection. Can you recall a time, for instance, when you were having a conversation and people were continuously walking by and disrupting your conversation, or when noisy fans or public address systems were blaring in the background? These things happen, and even when you recognize them as beyond your control, they can still make it difficult to connect with a person. There are only two solutions to external distractions:

1. Ignore them
2. Move elsewhere to continue

But what if your partner causes the distractions? Is he or she playing with something? Perhaps for her it's a piece of jewelry; for him, jingling the change in his pocket. Let's face it — we all have annoying habits, some more annoying than others. You need to absolutely ignore any such habits in your partner. Suspend your own likes and dislikes for the moment, or they will hinder your ability to connect.

But how to go about it?

1. Think about why you need to connect with this person, and why you must work together
2. Focus on what you want to accomplish and push out things that annoy you
3. Act as if your partner is the most important person in your life

You'll eventually forget about the distraction if you can maintain your concentration.

Alternatively, you might try asking your partner to stop doing whatever it is that's annoying you. Try explaining the effect it's having on the conversation. Either your partner agrees — or not. You really have no control over how your partner will respond. If it's with annoyance or even anger, your connection is broken, and there's not much you can do to regain it at that point.

STAY FOCUSED

Whenever I take a client for a business lunch, I always sit so that I face in a direction away from major distractions. Other customers, waiters and waitresses passing in the aisle, noise from the bar — all are distractions that can interrupt a business discussion. I try to minimize them as much as possible so I can remain focused on my prospect.

— **Peter**

THE DRIVER

Just do it!

There are four broad behavioral styles that allow us to determine the way a person is behaving at any moment. They also give us the ability to respond appropriately to a person's actions. These four styles are briefly outlined in *Differences*. Here is more on one of those styles.

The Driver is a high achiever — a mover and shaker who is definitely not averse to risk. This individual is extroverted, strong-willed, direct, practical, organized, forceful, and decisive. Look for someone who tells it the way it is and is very persuasive. Watch out or you'll be worn down and bowled over. A Driver is task-oriented rather than relationship-oriented and wants immediate results.

This individual is not concerned with *how* something is done, but *what* is being done, and *what* results can be expected. "What" is his or her battle cry. "What's going on? What's being done about it? What you should do is . . . !"

The Driver can be stubborn, domineering, impatient, insensitive, and short-tempered, with little time for formalities or niceties. He or she can also be demanding, opinionated, controlling, and uncompromising — or even overbearing, cold, and harsh.

The Driver's pleasure is power, control, and respect. His or her pain is loss of respect, lack of results, and the feeling that he or she is being taken advantage of.

When communicating with a Driver

— Support the person's need to be in control
— Focus on the task
— Talk about expected results
— Be businesslike and factual
— Provide concise, precise, and organized information
— Discuss and answer "what" questions
— Argue facts, not feelings
— Don't waste time
— Don't argue details
— Provide options

THE DRIVER . . . PORTRAIT OF AN OFFICE

Of course, it must be the corner office with two windows, but the Driver never looks at the view. Pictures on the wall are of battle-fields, maps, and boats. The Driver is a multi-tasked person and can sign letters, hold interviews, and talk on the phone simultaneously. Office furniture contributes to the impression of power and control, and is the most expensive and incredible available.

The office may also contain flowers and plants, even exotic ones like orchids (carefully chosen to contribute to the impression of power), but the Driver never looks after them. There's an assistant to do that. On the desk are often family portraits, but never candid shots. They are formal portraits showing everyone in his or her proper role, frozen forever as the Driver sees them. The office will probably be decorated by an interior designer to create the feeling of power, and the colors of the office will be strong power colors. Curt and tough, straight to business: that's the Driver at work in his or her den. Don't waste time. Get straight to the point! *Symbol:* Eagle.

— Peter

*E*FFECTIVE COMMUNICATORS

Throughout history, outstanding leaders have been ordinary people with extraordinary vision — and the skill to communicate it.

— PETER

Think of someone who you consider to be a good communicator. What makes that person effective? You'll probably find that three things do.

1. A positive attitude
2. A clearly defined goal
3. People skills

A *positive attitude* means that you approach what you want as though you can't fail. If you assume you'll fail before you start, that will communicate itself in your voice and actions. As Henry Ford once said, "Whether you think you can or whether you think you can't, you're probably right."

A *clearly defined goal* must not only be clear in your own mind, but must be linked to your listener's needs. In fact, your own goal must be something that your listener also needs, or believes he needs. People do things for *their* reasons, not yours. You must provide the benefits in order for your listener to act.

Finally, *people skills,* or communication skills, take practice and knowledge regarding how to proceed. These basic skills include self-awareness, self-control, self-motivation, an understanding of differences between people, and the ability to cope with the feelings of others.

LIGHTING THE SPARK

When Martin Luther King Jr. gave his unforgettable speech, "I have a dream that one day this nation will rise up and live out the true meaning of this creed; We hold these truths to be self-evident: that all men are created equal . . . " nothing could have more effectively communicated his vision of the future. In a sense, the rest is history. King's words galvanized a nation to action.

— Peter

EMOTION

It's normal to feel angry, frustrated, and let down by what others do. How you respond, however, is always up to you!
— ROBERT

Your emotions can both help and hinder communication. When you're communicating with another person, set aside your first reactions and suspend judgment for the moment. Find a way to control your emotions.

We live in a world of cause and effect, stimulus and response. Effective communicators create a pause between the stimulus (what someone does) and their response. A pause allows you to choose your best response.

When you react emotionally, you will breathe very shallowly and the muscles in your jaw, neck, and shoulders will tense up.

If you don't believe this, watch someone who is nervous, flustered, or angry. He will consistently show these signs. You need to counter this defensive response and keep the oxygen flowing to your brain.

How? Create an *anchor* — something that will cause you to breathe deeply and relax the tension in the jaw, neck, and shoulder area. A good anchor is squeezing the thumb and forefinger of your right hand together and imagining a stop sign. This image reminds you to breathe deeply and relax these muscles. It will take time to feel comfortable with your anchor — in fact, it may take up to three weeks of daily practice. Associate deep breathing and muscle relaxation with the stop sign anchor. Trigger this image whenever you squeeze your thumb and forefinger together. Use it every day, several times each day if you can — this will help you call on it under pressure.

IT HAPPENS TO ALL OF US

Once, while addressing a confrontational individual in a meeting, I could feel the hairs on the back of my neck beginning to rise and my face getting flushed. I was about to lose it when I triggered the stop sign anchor. In fact, I had to trigger it several times during that situation. I continued to breathe deeply and consciously relaxed my muscles. I chose the best responses I could based on this individual's comments. And then, when I asked for clarification and proof of his comments, *he* became flustered and lost his temper. I remained calm and watched (as did everyone else) as he started to raise his voice and look foolish.

— Robert

EMPATHY

*You can persuade someone much more easily by
aligning with his or her feelings than by trying to
convince with reason or logic.*
— PETER

Empathy differs from sympathy. Empathy acknowledges someone else's feelings as being real and valid for them — even though you do not feel the same way. Sympathy is a state of having similar feelings to someone else.

It is important to empathize with others, to acknowledge emotion without becoming emotional. This is especially true if you have bad news to deliver. Prepare your partner as much as you can. Say right up front that you have bad news for him. This gives your partner time to prepare for it physically.

For example: You must dismiss an employee.

As soon as he enters your office, say, "I have some bad news for you." Then tell him he's about to be dismissed, give him the reasons why, and ask if he has any questions. You can't feel what he feels, but you *can* acknowledge his emotion.

Take these concrete steps to defuse stress whenever you must deliver bad news to people or give them corrective feedback.

1. Choose the best time and place.
2. Prepare them by telling them what you're about to discuss.
3. Deliver the bad news or corrective feedback. If it's bad news, tell them the reasons, discuss how you can help, and legitimize their emotions. If you're delivering corrective feedback, you must include the specific behavior or situation creating the problem, the effect it has, and the possible consequences.
4. Check their perceptions of what's happened. Do they agree or understand?
5. Discuss options.
6. Follow up.

It works the other way, too. When an employee has a triumph, no matter how minor, acknowledge the effort. Recognize good behavior and the employee will feel even better about it. Recognition is the number-one motivator in North America. What is recognized and rewarded is repeated.

IT'S SIMPLE BUT IT'S NOT EASY

The first time I dismissed an employee was as devastating for me as it was for him. It was necessary, yet I fretted for days. I wanted to appear tough and hold firm, yet the look of disappointment on Rick's face caught me off guard. As we discussed his options, I found myself wishing it were me being fired instead of him. After all, Rick was a good employee; unfortunately, we no longer required his help. I believe to this day that my concern for his well-being helped us part more as friends than as employer and employee.

Show compassion — you'll feel better about yourself and others will feel less abandoned and alone.

— Robert

|ENVIRONMENT

Where you are and what's happening there has an effect on how you communicate — before you even open your mouth!
— ROBERT

When you connect with another person, whether at the office or at home, closely observe your partner's surroundings (assuming your partner has some control over them).

- How confident is your partner? It's common to be confident in one location, such as home, but not in another, such as a meeting.
- Is the environment neat and orderly or messy and disorganized?
- Does your partner appear thorough and meticulous?
- What is your partner interested in?
- Are there paintings on the wall?
- Are there certificates, degrees, or trophies?
- Are there photos of family, friends, or celebrities? Who are these people?
- What signs reflect your partner's status in the community or company?
- What is your partner's sphere of influence?

— What are your partner's interests?

— Is there sports equipment, or other indications of your partner's hobbies, interests, or background in the room?

Checking out and remembering such information about your partner helps you to connect and develop a more complete picture of him or her.

A FLY ON THE DESK IS WORTH TWO ON THE WALL

I remember so well working with a severe and reserved CEO who had nothing in his office that told me there might be something behind the business facade he wore so well. His office was meticulous — no photos, documents, certificates — nothing that could give me a clue to the personality of the man. As I worked with him frequently, this led to an uncertainty in our dealings that, while not hostile, was uncomfortable.

Then one day I noticed he had a small, brilliant fishing fly on his desk. It hadn't been there when I had visited him before. I knew nothing about flyfishing, but I commented on the brilliant colors of the fly and asked if he was a fisherman. Not only was he a fisherman, he had created that very fly. It was named after him.

I quickly asked a series of questions, and within minutes he was virtually pouring out his life history in fishing to me. It was a complete revelation. This austere man had such a passion for fishing that he could talk about it for hours — and he did. We formed a better connection and our future encounters were much more rewarding.

— Robert

EVALUATING

Have you ever noticed that the straightest stick is crooked in the water? In forming judgments of others, or in passing opinions upon current topics, let us go slow and be careful until we know all the existing circumstances.

— JOHN WANAMAKER

In *Empathy* we talk about a specific example of empathy. Here, we're more concerned with it as a component of the *HEART* formula. In *HEART*, "E" stands for *Empathize before you evaluate.*

Feelings are important because they determine how you and your partner perform in communication with each other. Listen for your partner's feelings and then evaluate the facts that support them.

Try to be hard on facts and easy on people. Be open-minded and accepting of others, even if you don't accept their ideas.

Curb your own opinions and emotions and listen fully to what your partner says, doesn't say, or indicates through body language and facial expression. Demonstrate your caring and understanding. Use his or her name. Respect silences and pauses.

Feel what your partner feels in order to understand the full message. Share in his or her joy, enthusiasm, pain, and sorrow. When you empathize with your partner's feelings, you experience the power behind the person's words.

Don't be too quick to offer solutions. Often, your partner just wants to vent. Let it happen and let your partner know she or he has been heard, understood, and appreciated. Empathy means entering fully, through imagination or experience, into another person's feelings and motives. Don't belittle those feelings or pass them off as insignificant. Use the facts to evaluate the validity of those feelings.

EMPATHIZE AND EVALUATE

The hardest thing about facts is to face them — and even when people agree on them, they often disagree on what they mean.

Most of us were excited about computerizing our practice. Jane, however, was troubled. Jane was the employee in charge of day-to-day operations. Why was she resistant? She didn't have the necessary computer skills or the desire to learn them. She was comfortable with the way things were and didn't want to change. Sound familiar?

By carefully questioning her concerns we discovered several fears, uncertainties, and doubts. Her poor academic background fueled her fear that she would be unable to learn the new skills — and that this would lead to her dismissal.

By surfacing these facts, clearly stating what we were prepared to do, and eliminating her faulty perceptions, we were in a better position to evaluate the situation. Having done this, we could choose the best approach to a resolution.

Evaluate the facts behind the feelings. The only things you have to lose are misunderstandings and misperceptions.

— Robert

THE EXPRESSIVE

Nothing is impossible for the one who doesn't have to do it himself.
— PETER

The Expressive, one of the four basic behavioral types outlined in *Differences,* is always at the center of the party.

A verbally adept personality, the Expressive is engaging, accommodating, supportive of others, persuasive, socially adept, and relationship-oriented rather than task-oriented. He or she loves to be one of the gang, and is always ready for something new and exciting, especially if the gang is ready to participate. Additional strengths include enthusiasm, diplomatic skills, and the ability to inspire others.

Weaknesses involve impatience, a tendency to generalize, verbal assaults, and sometimes irrational behavior. The Expressive can also be egotistical, manipulative, undisciplined, reactive, unorganized, and abrasive.

The Expressive readily exchanges information and life experiences. His main need is to be appreciated and accepted. The Expressive's pleasure is recognition and approval. His pain is isolation and lack of attention.

When communicating with an Expressive

— Focus on developing a relationship
— Try to show how your ideas will improve his or her image
— Be enthusiastic, open, and responsive
— Relate to the need to share information, stories, and experiences
— Be forthcoming and willing to talk
— Ask and answer "who" questions
— Remember to be warm and approachable at all times
— Work to minimize his or her direct involvement with details or personal conflicts

THE EXPRESSIVE . . . PORTRAIT OF AN OFFICE
In short, it's a mess. The Expressive loves favorite sayings and has them plastered on the wall or sitting on the desk. Files are never in a filing cabinet. Rather, they're piled all over the office in stacks. But don't be misled: The Expressive knows exactly where everything is and can find virtually anything by its location. Office colors will probably be loud and lively. If there are flowers or plants, they're likely dead — either talked to death or lacking water. The Expressive's greatest reward is personal acknowledgment from other people, and examples of this will be displayed. The Expressive is an excitable dreamer, with lots of ideas and projects, but without the time to follow them up. *Symbol:* Peacock.

— Peter

EYE CONTACT

Eyes, what are they? Colored glass,
Where reflections come and pass.
Open windows — by them sit
Beauty, Learning, Love, and Wit.
— MARY COLERIDGE

Surely one of the most clichéd and amusing comments in our language is the phrase "Look deep into my eyes . . . " It calls to mind every corny Hollywood movie ever made involving hypnotism. Yet there was a time when people didn't laugh. Mesmerism (or hypnotism, named after the Austrian physician Franz Mesmer) was very much associated with possession — the idea that the eye is the window of the soul, and that the soul could somehow be manipulated.

Today, there is still a great reluctance to gaze deeply into another's eyes (unless you are dating). Direct eye contact can be both threatening and "mesmerizing."

Of course, it's a good thing to maintain eye contact with your partner for direct communication, but there is actually no need to "gaze deep" into his or her eyes. Instead, you can *appear* to maintain eye contact. To do this, just look at the bridge of the nose and then slowly let your eyes scan around the person's face. From a distance of about three feet, which is close contact indeed, no one can tell whether you're looking at your

partner's left eye, right eye, nose, or chin — as long as your eyes don't fix-
ate on one place only.

Try not to blink too much, especially if you're in a potentially threatening situation. Blinking is often a sign of nervousness or fear, and if your
partner is perceptive, it's a dead giveaway to your emotions.

THE STARING GAME

Do you remember playing the staring game when you were a kid?
The object was to see who could stare longest at an adult without
being forced to turn away. I used to play the game with other kids
when I went to a restaurant. If we did it right, we could make
the adult very uncomfortable, wondering why he was being stared
at. Eye contact, even by children, is considered a challenge when
performed on a stranger. At the very least it's not polite. How often
do you remember your mother telling you, "Stop it! It's not polite
to stare!"?

— Peter

EYE MOVEMENT

By their shifting shall you know them.
— PETER

Through eye movements, you can tell if someone is drawing her answer to your question from the past, or if she is imagining it.

Consider this. Most of the time

— If the person is actually remembering an event, eye movements will be to the left
— If the person is creating the event in her imagination, eye movements will be to the right

These movements are known as "classical eye movements" and are true for about 90 percent of the population. The other 10 percent consistently reverse the eye movements; that is, left for creating the event, right for remembering it.

To tell if someone is lying, you must ask several questions to which you know the answers and watch the person's eyes. This will indicate that person's preference. Then ask a question to which you don't know the answer and watch if the eyes go in the same direction or the opposite direction. If they go in the opposite direction, the person is creating.

Other eye movements you can see involve the pupil (the black circle within the colored iris). Watch it for size changes. The pupil can dilate or contract:

— It will dilate when the person is involved in an intimate or interesting conversation
— It will contract as a person mentally "wanders" or is thinking about something else

LOOKING FOR SIGNALS

Many border-crossing guards are trained in observing eye movement. A border-crossing guard will ask you questions she can verify on her computer. "What's your name?" "Where do you live?" "How long have you been out of the country?" While you are answering, the guard "maps" your eye movements to see what direction they turn in. She will then ask you something she doesn't know the answer to. If your eyes go the other way, she becomes suspicious you're lying.

Trainers and speakers can use this knowledge as well. By moving to the right side of the platform, you draw your audience's eyes to the left and help them remember things in their past. By moving to the left, you draw their eyes to the right and help them be more creative. Amazing.

— Robert

*F*ACIAL LANGUAGE

If I had to choose whether to focus on the body or the face — I'd focus on the face.
— ROBERT

What is a person's emotional state: angry, sad, surprised, happy, fearful, or disgusted? Dr. Paul Ekmar at the University of California has developed a facial-action coding system by identifying six emotional expressions that are universally recognized. Here is a brief description of the facial gestures associated with these states.

1. Sadness — raised eyebrows with a wrinkled forehead
2. Surprise — raised eyebrows with an open mouth
3. Anger — lowered eyebrows with intent staring and bared teeth
4. Happy — smiling in the mouth and eye area, mouth open
5. Fear — wide open eyes and mouth with raised eyebrows
6. Disgust — wrinkled nose and open mouth

THE SCREAM

What could be more evocative than Edward Munch's great painting of human agony entitled "The Scream"? In it an individual, obviously at the total end of his or her psychological resources, is pictured on a bridge with eyes and mouth wide open. Everything about the person indicates psychological fear and anguish.

Remember that famous photograph of Kim Phuc, a young Vietnamese girl who had just survived a napalm attack on June 8, 1972? Kim, who now lives in Canada, shows the same face of fear. The gestures are so alike that Kim's image could be substituted for the face in Munch's painting. Her facial gestures, as well as the wide distribution of the photo, played a major role in bringing the bitter Vietnamese conflict to an end. Universally recognized gestures alone can move us to understanding and action.

— **Robert**

FEELINGS

*People will not listen to facts until you have acknowl-
edged their feelings.*
— ROBERT

One of the most important rules of good communica-
tion is to focus on your partner's emotional and mental state. We are all
emotional by nature. We act emotionally and only then do we find the
logic to justify our actions. If you want to connect, you must first
acknowledge the validity of feelings.

Perceptions create feelings, feelings create thoughts, and thoughts
create behaviors.

— Does your partner appear distracted or upset?
— Is your partner concerned for his or her well-being?
— Can you put your finger on your partner's emotional assumptions?
— Is your partner elated or angry?

Look at the situation from your partner's point of view. Ask yourself,
"How would I feel if I was this person in this situation?"

TO ERR CAN BE HUMILIATING

One day, I was giving a seminar on Power Presentations. I had a small group and there was one man sitting in the front who looked like he had fallen asleep (and I hate snoozers). At the break I went to him and suggested he go home because he looked too tired to stay in the session. He looked at me and said, "Yes, my wife just died three days ago." After that I merely said humbly, "Look, I'm sorry. Just sit here and if you get something out of my session, great. If not, don't worry about it."

— **Peter**

FETA

Say what you have to say, but say it concisely, completely, and congruently.
— ROBERT

It's time to state your thoughts, feelings, and expectations. They are yours, so remember to use the word "I." To do otherwise implies that they belong to someone else, creates defensiveness in your partner, and reduces your credibility.

Give the person a "cheesy" response — *FETA*.

F eelings
E xpectations
T houghts
A greement

State how you feel about the situation or the person's behavior. Tell him or her your thoughts about the effects it will have and the consequences involved. Propose your expectations or solutions, then see if the person agrees. If your partner doesn't, then negotiate a way that is acceptable to both of you.

KNOW WHAT YOU WANT

It was 4:30 p.m. and my hotel room hadn't been cleaned. This is what I said:

"I'm disappointed (feelings).

"I would like a discount on my room (expectations) because it's 4 p.m., the bed isn't made, and my room is untidy (my thoughts).

"Can you do this for me?"

The hotel sent someone to tend to the room and credited my account with one free night. You get more of what you want when you know what it is and how to ask for it.

— **Robert**

HOLISTIC LISTENING

Listening is a magnetic and strange thing, a creative force. You can see that when you think how the friends that really listen to us are the ones we move toward, and we want to sit in their radius as though it did us good, like ultraviolet rays.

— BRENDA UELAND

Holistic listeners combine empathetic listening with analytical listening and integrate what they hear to achieve win/win outcomes. Most importantly, they take the time to connect and listen. They use what is said and not said, what they feel, what they know, and everything else at hand to improve their understanding of the person and the situation.

Holistic listeners can separate concrete information from opinions and enthusiasm from evidence. They are capable of weighing facts and feelings — and digression or repetition doesn't faze them. They acknowledge people and their ideas and don't deny them their feelings. They don't fight to be right, offer advice, or lecture others.

Most importantly, holistic listeners don't prejudge.

Prejudging is a form of listening in which the listener has already determined what he or she expects to hear, and then selectively listens for evidence to support that view. Once the listener hears what is expected, there is a determined attempt to shut down their communication partner by using judgmental comments such as "I thought so," or "That's ridiculous," or even "Uh-oh . . . here it comes!"

LISTENING BY INSTINCT

Facts without understanding are as dangerous as a car without steering or brakes. Understanding comes from weighing all the evidence.

Jim said he understood what I wanted. A gnawing feeling inside me told me he really didn't. You can call that feeling an instinct, an intuition, or an upset stomach. You can call it whatever you want, but it is part of the information that leads to a better understanding of the situation.

By carefully questioning Jim's understanding of my desired outcome, I realized that he *thought* he understood what I was asking for, but he really didn't. I re-explained what I expected in a different way and focused on my expectations and desired outcome.

Jim finished the project on time in the way we had discussed. We were both pleased with the outcome.

Don't bias your understanding by selectively focusing on only part of the message. Use everything — what's said, what's not said, body language, experience . . .

— Robert

*I*NTERRUPTIONS

Welcome interruptions — on your terms, not theirs.
— ROBERT

Sometimes it's hard to get things done because of all the interruptions. There are many things you can do to prevent interruptions — close your door, refrain from establishing eye contact, or leave the building, to mention three. But what if someone has already interrupted you? What should you do then?

Ask yourself, "Is this more important than what I'm doing now?" If the answer is "yes," stop what you're doing, stand up, and focus on the person. If the answer is "no," then stand up and reschedule a meeting for later. (To find out more on the benefits of standing up, see the anecdote at the end of this chapter, "Foiling Interruptions.")

This is how you do it:

1. Get the person's attention by using his or her name.
2. Acknowledge what they've said by summarizing it.
3. Explain your situation.
4. Reschedule to meet with the person later.

FOILING INTERRUPTIONS

Unfortunately, when you need something, it's an emergency. When someone else needs it, it's an interruption. As unfair as this seems, sometimes you're just too busy to handle someone else's needs at that particular point in time.

Try this the next time someone comes into your office and you don't have time to talk. Stand up. Walk around your desk to greet them. Stay standing while you talk. In fact, don't even have extra chairs in your office. Don't let them plant their "you-know-what" and you won't have to dig it out.

There's nothing more uncomfortable than having to stand for extended periods of time. This shortens the amount of time that people will spend in your office. In fact, barring exceptional situations, they might even stop dropping by. As a result, you'll be able to get more work accomplished.

— **Robert**

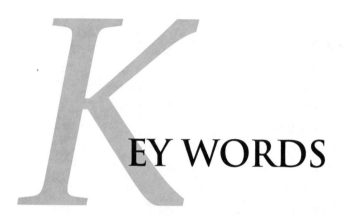

KEY WORDS

A word is dead when it is said, some say.
I say it just begins to live that day.
— EMILY DICKINSON

If you notice someone repeating himself, chances are he doesn't feel you got it, so acknowledge him by reflecting back his key words and phrases.

Key words and phrases differ from sensory words and phrases. They have very little to do with how someone *processes information* (see the sections on visual, auditory, and kinesthetic methods outlined in this book), and everything to do with the *specific meanings* words have attached to them. Of the five hundred words most commonly used in the English language, each has an average of 28 different meanings.

There are four techniques that will help you use key words.

1. Use your partner's name. It holds attention, shows respect, and is a powerful way to connect.
2. Use simple, understandable words. Speak to express, not impress. Avoid jargon, clichés, and terms that may confuse your partner. If you must use jargon, make sure your partner understands what the

words you are using mean.

3. Use "we," "us," and "our." Move from "I" and "you" to "we" and "us." Show you're working with your partner. This one simple step can quickly align you as equals facing similar situations and problems. These words make you collaborative and cooperative right away.

4. Reflect your partner's key words and phrases to acknowledge that you've heard them.

Here's an example. You have delegated a task to a subordinate. The subordinate comes to you with a problem. You ask, "What do *you* see as some possible solutions?" If the subordinate replies with some potential solutions, ask which he thinks are the most workable. Once the solutions have been narrowed to one or two, reply, "I see. *We* could probably implement those. What else do *we* need so *we* can still get our project done on time and budget?"

You have helped your subordinate think the problem through and propose possible solutions. You might have guided his thinking in the process, yet the responsibility remained solely with him to propose the solutions. Then you let him know that he wasn't alone. By using the word "we," you aligned with him and offered him support by referring to the project as one shared between the two of you.

WORDS MATTER, BUT DON'T GET HUNG UP ON THEM

Sometimes the meaning you give to a word is different from the meaning your listener interprets. If the disagreement seems fundamental, it might help to change your terminology. If you do, and the disagreement vanishes, then the problem was what we call *semantic*, meaning that it was with the words only. If the problem doesn't disappear, likely the disagreement is fundamental, and it will be necessary to redefine your terms so you are both operating with the same vocabulary.

Here's an example of this. Once during a seminar, a participant disagreed with me on the topic of kinesthetic learning, which is learning through feelings and doing. She felt that what I was talking about was intuition. To solve the problem, I asked her if intuition is the same as instinct. She said no. I then asked whether acting on one's feelings is similar to acting on intuition. She thought it might be. So then I suggested that the three main senses used for learning in North America are vision, hearing, and intuition (instead of feelings). She accepted that.

Don't get hung up on the words. Focus on the message.

— **Robert**

KINESTHETIC WORDS

And now we come to the magic of words. A word, also, just like an idea, a thought, has the effect of reality upon undifferentiated minds.
— EMMA JUNG

As we indicate in *Sensory Words,* different types of people express themselves in and respond to different types of words, depending on the way they perceive the world around them. Kinesthetic people relate to the world through their physical and emotional feelings. You can recognize kinesthetic people by their use of words such as the following, and you can use words like these to get your ideas across to them.

Attack	Handle	Let it go
Charge your batteries	Hands-on	Off balance
Cold	Hold on	Perception
Crash	Insight	Play
Dig	Instinct	Play with it
Dig into it	Intuition	Press the issue
Feel right	It'll take off soon	Pressure
Fumble	It's shaping up	Rough
Grasp	Know-how	Run with

Sense	Stoop to her level	Touch
Sharp as a tack	Support	Try it on
Smooth	Tickle	Vibes
Solid	Tickle your fancy	Warm

HANDLING A KINESTHETIC PERSPECTIVE

Think back to our examples in *Auditory Words* on page 30. If your partner responded with, "I've got a firm grasp of the details. Let's get going," then that person is responding from a kinesthetic perspective.

Your best response might be, "Great! I'll be around if you *feel* you need any *support*. Let's *touch base* next week — why don't we *pencil in* for Tuesday at 4 p.m.?"

— Robert

KNOW-IT-ALLS

It's not what you know that's the problem, it's what you think you know that just ain't so!
— MARK TWAIN

We've all met difficult characters. They can't be avoided, so we have to deal with them. Here are some suggestions on dealing with one of the better-known types — the Know-it-all.

Know-it-alls come in two varieties: the true Know-it-all and the Think-they-know-it-all. The true Know-it-all is knowledgable and competent. The problem is that he can also be single-minded, condescending, and closed-minded.

Here are some tips on dealing with the true Know-it-all:

— Be sure what you say is accurate
— Ask more than you tell
— Propose hypothetical scenarios to challenge assumptions
— Be indirect and reflect what the person has said
— Listen and acknowledge
— Stand up to condescending tones and accusations
— Keep your ego quiet — seek the person's opinion

The Think-they-know-it-all craves attention. Here are some tips on dealing with the Think-they-know-it-all:

— Listen to give the person the attention she or he wants
— Ask for specifics
— State the facts as you know them
— Allow the person to save face
— Reference other sources and opinions

THE BEST KIND OF KNOW-IT-ALL

The bigger a man's head, the easier it is to fill his shoes — or so the saying goes. When two Know-it-alls meet, it's a case of an "I" for an "I."

Wendy had all the answers. Fortunately, she never allowed her superior intellect and knowledge to go to her head — so to speak. She had a super personality and was always willing to help out. She made her point without making you feel inferior or dumb. If only all Know-it-alls possessed her people skills.

Know-it-alls are a gift if they possess such good people skills. If they don't possess them, teach them. Fake Know-it-alls want attention. Give it to them by focusing on their strengths.

— Robert

*L*EADERSHIP

The greatest discovery of this generation: Human beings can alter their lives by altering their attitudes.
— WILLIAM JAMES

When two people communicate, one has to be the leader. This is not always the person who is doing the talking. Communication leadership can be obtained through asking questions, tone, and body language. In effective communication, the "leadership" switches back and forth from one partner to the other.

That's the simple way of stating something that's fairly complex. The key is to be a good leader, and leadership comes from within. It involves

— Knowing yourself
— Having vision and passion
— Taking risks
— Being able to communicate effectively
— Being aware of your progress and the results you get

These are known as the five key steps to personal and professional leadership from within, a system now used in many companies and leading universities. For more information and instructions, consult *Leadership from Within* by Peter Urs Bender (see *Recommended Reading*).

PADDLE THE CANOE TOGETHER

Contained in *Leadership from Within* are the instructions to "paddle your own canoe." Follow the program and your life will "come about" in the fashion you want it to.

In real life, however, when two people are together on a mission, one of them has to be the leader. Think of two people in a canoe. One's in the bow, the other in the stern. They both have to paddle in unison (although with different paddling styles) for the canoe to go anywhere. The bow person adds power to the stroke. The stern controls the rudder, but the bow person can make the rudder react quickly or slowly. Cooperation is the only way to proceed. When that cooperation is generous and voluntary, the canoe can travel at astonishing speeds.

— Peter

LISTENING

Listen to everyone in your company, especially the ones who actually talk to customers. They really know what's going on out there.
— SAM WALTON

Listening means fully and completely understanding your partner. You don't have to agree with what you hear, but you *must* understand what was said. Listening involves hearing, seeing, and feeling. Active listening requires active participation and involves supportive gestures, questions, verbalizations ("mm-hmm," "ohh," "ahh"), and encouraging words such as "really," "oh no," and "tell me more."

We all have an innate need to be heard. We cry out for it. We want to be appreciated, respected, and acknowledged.

Think of a time when you felt fully listened to and understood. How did you feel? Fulfilled? Satisfied? Content? Possibly all that and more.

Now think of a time when your partner didn't pay attention. Perhaps he or she was just waiting for you to finish speaking, or worse, waiting to cut you off. How did you feel? Irritated? Frustrated? Combative? You're not alone.

Good listeners are patient, flexible, and open-minded. They are interested in their partners and are often thought to be great conversationalists because they can disagree without being disagreeable or insensitive. They disagree after having understood your point of view, and they do so tactfully.

Poor listeners, on the other hand, always seem to rush the conversation. They are often considered intolerant, disagreeable, and insensitive. They wait impatiently to speak, cut others off, and focus only on themselves and what they consider important.

It's estimated that 60 percent of all corporate problems stem from poor listening. Workers claim that managers just don't listen. Managers claim that workers' biggest problem is they just don't follow directions. Study after study shows employee motivation can be substantially increased simply by listening.

And what about marriages? How often have you heard the phrase, "He/She just doesn't listen to me!" Poor listening is the excuse most often cited for marital breakdowns.

Poor listening is costly, too. If you accept the thesis that poor listening and misunderstanding can account for poor workmanship, it's possible each person could cost your company $10 in time and wasted resources each week. With ten employees, the cost to the company could be $100 a week, $400 a month, or $4,800 a year. With 100 employees, the listening error could run to $1,000 a week, $4,000 a month, or $48,000 a year. This is big money regardless of the size of your company.

Like driving a car, listening is under your control. How you control your listening determines where you and your partner will end up in your communication venture.

Listening is a skill that has to be learned; yet it is perhaps the most underrated, underutilized, and underdeveloped interpersonal skill. It is at the core of every successful human interaction, and if you work with or for others, it's an absolute must.

Great listeners are interactive, involved, and focused. Good listening requires concentration, effort, and active participation, and it expends energy.

Think of yourself as a vacuum extracting every bit of information from your partner so you can better understand and evaluate the message.

LISTEN TO SUCCEED

The golden rule of listening is to listen to others as you would have them listen to you.

Ben Feldman was the first insurance salesman to surpass $25 million in one year — in fact, he proceeded to double that. He did this in East Liverpool, a small town of 20,000 people on the Ohio River. When asked his secret, he said,

- Work hard
- Think big
- Listen very well

Apply the golden rule of listening and try this: Listen more than you talk.

— Robert

MARKETING YOURSELF

You might market yourself poorly. You might market
yourself well. But you cannot not market.
— Peter Urs Bender and George Torok

Marketing may seem a strange topic for a book on
interpersonal communication. But when you are communicating with
another individual you are, in fact, "marketing" yourself and your ideas
to that person. In its broadest sense, marketing can be conscious or
unconscious. Conscious marketing involves all the steps you take to
sell your ideas. But unconscious marketing may determine how someone
perceives you before you even open your mouth.

In a few words, marketing

— Expresses who you are
— Defines what you do
— Creates a perception of your value

Marketing is not just about projecting a successful image for your
company. It's about projecting a successful image of yourself — and
controlling the perceptions that people have about you.

For more information and a host of suggestions, see *Secrets of Power Marketing* by Peter Urs Bender and George Torok (see *Recommended Reading*).

TWO STYLES OF MARKETING

Consider two of the world's greatest artists: Vincent van Gogh and Pablo Picasso. Today, their paintings are worth millions. They are celebrated and renowned masters of their craft. But how successful were they when they were alive?

Van Gogh was a genius at painting. However, he was also very introverted and shy. He couldn't talk to people. As a result, he was a total failure at communication and never managed to promote himself or his work. He died a frustrated and nearly penniless man.

Picasso, on the other hand, was good at both. He was not afraid to express himself and be noticed. He wore big hats. He was a showman. He was able to sell his ideas. Despite the fact that Picasso's artistic style was ahead of his time, he was very successful during his life because he was an excellent communicator.

— Peter

MATCHING

The gesture is the thing truly expressive of the individual — as we think so will we act.
— MARTHA GRAHAM

Our unconscious gestures reveal more than we imagine. Body language is the single most important way we communicate besides spoken language itself. In a sense, how we move is even more telling than what we say, because body language is often unconscious and it's very difficult to control in an active way. But it can be done.

It's important to be aware of the unconscious messages our partner is sending us in the form of facial gestures, body language, and other movements. These motions offer us a wonderful way to connect.

Body language varies widely between people. Some are very animated, while others barely move at all. Some are very expressive, while others have true poker faces. But everybody has some body language. The trick is to match your partner's body language.

How to do it? If you are in sync with someone, you naturally do the following things. Use these techniques to match your partner.

— Slowly and confidently assume a similar body posture, rhythm, or gesture. When your partner sits, you might sit. When he stands, you might stand. When he leans, you might lean. The whole idea is to adjust — over time — to a similar position, gesture, or motion.

— Become aware of the amount of eye contact you should share. Follow your partner's lead. Too much eye contact might be threatening. Too little might make you appear shifty. Seek a balance by using your partner as a guide.

— Try to blend in with your partner's dress code. Dress as well as expected and if you're unsure, err on the conservative side. Always ask yourself, "Does my dress enhance my position or detract from it?" Your goal is to be seen as respectful, considerate, and professional.

NO WORDS NEEDED TO START A CONVERSATION

I once started a conversation with someone I didn't know, in a park, without saying a word. He sat alone on a park bench. I observed his posture and matched it. He opened the conversation.

— **Robert**

MISMATCHING

In face-to-face communication, just as in a phone
conversation, you eventually need to disconnect.
Do it gracefully, but do it firmly.
— ROBERT

Mismatching is the technique you use when you deliberately want to "disconnect." It's something we do most of the time quite naturally. But sometimes being conscious of the fact that you want to quit the conversation can help you do it more gracefully.

Mismatching your partner's words, vocal qualities, or body language is an effective technique to subtly send a message that the meeting is over. Use non-sensory-specific words, change your rate of speech, turn away, or lose eye contact. Don't be rude, but don't hesitate to use these techniques to end a meeting or a conversation.

IT'S TIME TO GO

I find the best way of ending a conversation that is going nowhere, or a meeting that has served its purpose, is to simply say, "I've got to go now." If you want to expand on the closure you can plead time restraints, or pressure of work, or a dozen other things that might occur to you. But small excuses will get you nowhere if you do not announce quite clearly that the meeting, or the communication, has ended.

— Peter

MISTRUST

Treat people the way they would like to be treated and they will treat you well.
— PETER

If empathy can create a bond of trust, betrayal can create a situation that may destroy any feeling of trust between communicating partners — perhaps forever.

Have you ever confided something to someone that you didn't want others to know . . . and then found that the confidence had been betrayed? How did you feel? Would you ever confide in that person again?

The problem goes deeper than betrayal of confidence. Perhaps an employee confides a personal problem to a co-worker, or discloses an abuse problem. Not only may the co-worker forfeit the person's trust if he reveals this publicly — but the act may also trigger an angry backlash, perhaps even litigation. The daily news is full of stories of employees who felt slighted and demeaned by confidences betrayed and who took legal action to vent their anger. This is equally true in your personal relationships.

SOME COMMENTS ARE IRREVERSIBLE

Jim knew his marriage was over the moment an acquaintance repeated what he had told his wife in strict confidence. It was a blow that drove home the fact that Jim could no longer trust his wife to guard his secret wishes and concerns.

It takes months, even years, to establish mutual trust — and only one careless slip to lose it.

Be careful — very careful — to maintain a confidence. If one person can't trust you, can anyone? Keep secrets secret. Your name and character depend on it. They are your most important assets.

— Robert

MISUNDER-STANDING

You have two ears, two eyes, and one mouth.
Use them in those proportions.
— ROBERT

Misunderstanding results partially from a speaker's in-ability to make his thoughts clear for you. But it can also arise when you as a listener don't express *yourself* effectively, and therefore are unable to help the speaker help you understand. You can't control how your partner speaks, but you *can* control how you participate in the communication process. Active participation will greatly increase your chances of successfully understanding the message, no matter how distorted it seems to come out.

Tom Peters, a business author and speaker, once said, "There is no real-ity, only perception." Conflict, or misunderstanding, arises because we selectively hear, filter, and retain what we hear, see, and feel — to corre-spond to our view of the world.

When you listen passively, you can quickly misunderstand the speaker's message. You filter and distort the message to suit your needs.

Filtering is selective hearing. It makes what you hear fit your percep-tion of reality. That's why you pay attention only to what you consider important.

Distortion occurs when you focus on the details of the message and ignore the bigger picture. If you dislike or distrust your partner, you will distort what is said even more.

Think of a satellite dish. You are the receiver, and the signal is your partner's message. Sometimes the signal is strong and clear. Other times it isn't. When the signal is blocked, distortion occurs. Selective hearing and other obstructions block understanding.

Misunderstanding is normal in face-to-face communication. We filter out 70 percent to 90 percent of what we hear and 48 hours later, we retain only a fraction of that. Like the satellite receiver, we need to reach out for the "intended" meaning.

IT'S NOT WHAT SHE SAYS THAT MATTERS

Imagine a co-worker speaking to you after a meeting. She asks you what its purpose was. "They didn't need us. They should have just sent us an email. No one even cared to ask our views," she rages.

You reply, "Well, they likely did it that way because they wanted to give us the information directly and felt a meeting was the best way to do it."

Even if you're right, you've done the wrong thing. Your co-worker wasn't looking for an explanation; she was looking for acknowledgement.

A better reply might have been, "You're right! They could have given us that information in an email. You sound as though you would have liked to offer some suggestions. What would you have suggested they do differently?"

This acknowledgment of her need to express her views lays a much stronger foundation for understanding. Had you not wanted to pursue it further, you might simply have replied, "Hmm, that's true," and carried on.

— **Robert**

| MOTIVATING

Motivation results from unfulfilled needs.
— PETER

Knowing how to motivate others is crucial to successfully influencing other people. In face-to-face communication, you want to focus on questions that will help you discover what motivates the person you're speaking to.

We'll do anything to avoid pain or gain pleasure, although the desire to avoid pain is often more powerful than the desire to gain pleasure. Questioning about this is a first step to understand how the individual is motivated.

Is the person motivated by wanting to avoid pain? ("I want to quit smoking because I'm afraid I'll get lung cancer.")

Or is the person motivated by pleasure? ("When I quit smoking my food will taste better!")

When you want to influence someone's opinion, you must get him or her into a receptive state. You get someone into this state by changing the person's mental focus and/or physical state.

The physical state is what a person is doing.

The mental focus is what a person is thinking about.

Have you noticed how difficult it is to start something rolling? Pushing a car is an example. It takes a lot to get it moving, but once it starts, it gains momentum and becomes easier to push.

This is also true of people. In order to overcome inertia, you must physically move the person. Changing a person's physical location will change a person's mental position.

Try it. Change the person's present activity. If she is sitting, have her stand. If she is writing, ask her to stop and get something for you. Suggest you take a walk together, perhaps just moving to another room. Once you've moved the person physically, try to get her to refocus her thoughts.

This process works personally as well. For instance: You are trying to write a letter. Nothing comes. You feel drained of ideas. No matter what you do, nothing happens. Get up. Go for a coffee or a tea. When you come back to your task, your mind seems to be working again. It is. You changed your physical state to allow yourself to refocus.

Another way to change a person's mental state is to ask him questions. First, however, ask yourself whether the person is proactive or reactive by nature. Proactive people are motivated to act on their own. Reactive people generally wait until they absolutely have to act.

Here are a few examples of questions to ask your partner:

— What is important about . . . ?
— How would you handle . . . ?
— What would it take to get your support on this?
— What do you look for in a . . . ?

What you will get in reply are important motivation criteria — in short, what is important to the individual. Try to remember the exact words and use them when you respond. The individual will thus know that he has been heard and understood.

The next question you ask should be "Why is having (insert partner's own criteria) important to you?" Your partner can only answer in one of two ways: *toward* something or *away* from something. Focus on helping your partner move toward or away from what is wanted. For instance, moving toward wealth is different from moving away from poverty. The two may seem similar at the conscious level but are completely different at the unconscious level.

Then ask, "How will you know when you have (insert partner's own criteria)?" Again, the person will answer in one of two ways.

First, your partner may just say she just "knows." Such people are *internally motivated* and will need little support or recognition from you or others.

Second, your partner might reply that family, colleagues, or the boss would indicate whether she was successful through their reactions to the results. These people are *externally motivated* and will need recognition and acknowledgment as signs of success.

You could then ask, "How do (insert partner's own criteria) compare with what you have now, or perhaps with what you want in the future?" Again, the response will take one of two possible forms. It will be *different* or *the same*. You are motivated either to achieve things that are different from what you have, or to keep things the same as you already have, with perhaps a few modifications.

Finally, ask, "Why did you choose (insert partner's own criteria)?" Your partner will either list the exact steps in the process, or he will tell you a story about *how*, rather than *why*, he chose his present or current criteria.

If he answered the question "why" as it was asked, he wants a list of the options available. You could offer two or three options on how to proceed, and leave it up to the individual to go on from there.

If he answered as though you had asked a "how" question, he wants to know the exact steps or procedures to follow. You would then give the sequence he needs to proceed.

Asking questions like these helps you discover what it would take to motivate someone to move toward (or away) from what you want. The trick is to link what you want to his or her criteria and motivation needs.

Remember: In the simplest terms, we are motivated by anything that will give us pleasure or help us avoid pain. Some of us want money and tangible things; others want recognition and intangible rewards. Good listeners listen for those pains and pleasures.

If you're asking about your partner's pains, and your partner is focused on avoiding pain, you're not hearing what's important to him. Strive to understand the *who* behind the *what*. If you want one thing and your partner wants something else, you face a potential roadblock.

For instance: Imagine an upcoming decision regarding the purchase of some equipment for your department.

Your boss is stalling because she wants her decision to be perfect. She wants you to research it more.

You're impatient because you know there's no perfect piece of equipment. You just want it purchased and up and running, because time and money are being wasted with all the ongoing research.

You both have the same goal, but your motivations in the buying decision differ. This is when careful listening will help you. Your persuasion efforts might better focus on the cost of delaying the decision to offset the minimal difference that exists between the types of equipment available.

WHEN YOU'RE HUNGRY, YOU'RE MOTIVATED

Motivation results from unfulfilled needs. You've just spent two hours at a brunch buffet, and someone asks you what you'd like tonight for dinner. What do you think your answer will be? You will probably have no idea what you'd like for dinner. The reason for this is that your need for food has been fulfilled, and you're not motivated to think about anything else at that moment.

— Peter

NEGATIVE PEOPLE

That will never work!

There are two things that cannot be blatantly attacked: ignorance and narrow-mindedness. They can only be shaken by the simple development of the contrary qualities. "They will not bear discussion" — so mused Lord Acton more than a century ago.

No People are inherently negative. It is a learned behavior and is often rewarded in the workplace. Negative thinking projects the worst-case scenario. The problem with this is that truly negative people never participate in the "what-if" brainstorming, also known as "Pollyanna thinking." Worse yet, they rarely support change or help make changes work. Most negative people feel they are victims of circumstance and control is beyond their grasp.

Here are some tips on how to deal with negative people:

— Use their talent to unveil the worst-case scenarios.
— Get them involved in finding solutions by playing "what-if" games.
— Shield yourself from getting bogged down in their swamp of

negativity — it's more contagious than enthusiasm.

— Stick to specifics, not generalities.

— Create a list of "can-do's" and "can't-do's" with them, and let them choose from the list.

— Get a commitment as to what they intend to do.

— Help them deal with getting their life unstuck — help them find some joy.

— Be prepared to do without them or to clearly state your expectations of them.

Frequently, negative workers focus on the past (see *Time Differences*). "We never did it that way before" is one expression you'll often hear from them. Their logic is often confused, too. They may feel that since past changes brought no significant benefit to them, no significant benefit is likely to occur with more changes.

You have a few approaches to choose from when you are faced with this scenario.

1. Don't argue. You'll never win.
2. Be optimistic and do your homework.
3. Try to show them the benefits of past changes, if any.
4. Gradually swing them into the future by playing "what-if." "I know you don't believe this will work (already you're in the future tense), but *what if* it did? What would things be like then?" By forcing them to confront the *possibility* of something *yet to happen* you've already got them thinking in future terms, and out of the negative past-referencing.

ACCENTUATE THE POSITIVE

In the olden days, I believed you should walk away from negative people. Today I believe you should run away, because negative attitudes are contagious and can kill you just like the plague.

— Peter

NEGATIVES INTO POSITIVES

It doesn't matter if your glass is half full or half empty,
as long as it holds more than you can drink.
— ROBERT

Some find the positive in every situation. Others see the negative. It's all a matter of perspective. Positive connection happens most easily where there is mutual respect and the players are considered competent, credible, and trustworthy. But what happens when that isn't the case? What if you don't like the other person or the other person doesn't like you, especially if you're in a business situation and absolutely have to communicate with him or her?

- Find a positive thing, or preferably several, to say about the person. No one you deal with in real life is all bad.
- You must make the effort to share with that person. When two people dislike each other intensely, one of them must take the first step toward defusing the situation. The only one you can be sure to rely on is yourself.

SOMETIMES THE EFFORT IS TOUGH

For years there was animosity between me and my co-worker, Linda. I could not stand her slyness. She could not stand my brashness. It poisoned the working atmosphere and pained our colleagues and friends, many of whom we held in common. I could not understand what they saw in her. She could not understand what they saw in me. One New Year's, I made a single resolution. I could not allow our relationship to continue this way.

So I shoved the mass of enmity behind me and on January 2, I approached her and said, "I'm sorry for causing you such pain all these years. This is a new year. I truly would like to try again and put my animosity behind me. Will you help me?"

She could not accept my overture at first, and met me with open disbelief. But I had determined I would not let old enmities dictate my actions, and slowly, reluctantly, she began to be less hostile. One day she said to me, "I can't believe how you've changed towards me. Why?" I said I was simply unable to continue to hold her in contempt, and was trying to see her as I knew all our colleagues saw her — and that was a much better person than I had ever believed or seen before.

She started to cry. I was dumbfounded. She sobbed that no one, no one had ever said anything like that to her before. I asked her if she could trust me far enough to have regular discussions with me about things that bugged her. She said she would, and she did.

She became not necessarily a friend, but no longer an enemy. We were able to coexist with peace and honor. It was a lesson for both of us — one we often, individually and together, applied in our working environment.

— **Robert**

NON-VERBAL COMMUNICATION

Meanings are in people, not in their words.
— ROBERT

It's easier to change your words than to hide your intentions. Your words might disguise your intent, but not your subconscious physical responses. By itself, a single gesture means nothing. Meaning comes from reading your partner's overall impression and combining it with what is being said.

Non-verbal communication, or NVC, includes

- Body language
- Posture
- Gestures
- Eye contact
- Space
- Facial expressions
- Movements
- Tone of voice

In 1872, Charles Darwin noted that our ability to signal feelings, needs, and desires was critical to our survival. NVC reveals the truth more accurately than words. Studies confirm that it is more reliable, more accurate, and more informative than what is said.

While NVC is influenced by culture, it remains to some degree universal and universally recognizable. People from different parts of the world, for instance, can all identify six basic emotions (see also *Facial Language*):

1. Anger
2. Fear
3. Sadness
4. Disgust
5. Surprise
6. Happiness

Misunderstanding is common because we focus too intently on hearing what is said, and not observing and understanding non-verbal communication. The greater your awareness of NVC, the more powerful a communicator you will become.

BELIEVE THEIR NVC

She said she was fine — but her NVC said otherwise. Her voice was hesitant, weak, and on the verge of breaking. She was slouched in her chair, wringing her hands, and had a slight quiver in her lips. Judy appeared distant and couldn't look me in the eye.

Judy was suffering a tremendous strain, yet was unwilling to open up and share what it was. I looked at her and asked if I could help. She again said it was nothing. I knew her too well. I asked again. She started to cry and said her husband had just been diagnosed with cancer. Don't let someone's words fool you.

— Robert

OBJECTIVES

The greatest problem in communication is the illusion that it has been accomplished.
— George Bernard Shaw

Why do you need a clear outcome, goal, or objective? Because if you don't have a definite purpose in mind, you'll never know if you were persuasive or influential with your partner. Finding that goal is not always easy, however. The following questions may help you.

1. What do I hope happens as a result of this conversation?
2. What is my main point?
3. What will the other person need to know?
4. What can I do for the other person to entice him or her to help me?
5. Why is the meeting important?
6. What does the other person already know about my topic?

Every conversation should have an objective, even if it's simply to enjoy the conversation. Clarity is the key here. Many people can tell you what they don't want, but can't seem to focus on what they do want. Some know what they want, but can't state it clearly. To communicate successfully, you must have a clear objective in mind.

So the next time you set a goal, measure it against this simple formula, and you'll be more likely to achieve your objective in the end. These are the components of your goal or objective that must be communicated. Make your objectives *SMART*.

S   *pecific*
M   *easurable*
A   *ttainable*
R   *ealistic*
T   *imed*

The following are three situations that make people change.

1. A catastrophe such as sudden poor health, war, or a natural disaster
2. Finding the "right" religion, "a light going on at the end of the tunnel"
3. A *SMART* objective

You have the option to wait till catastrophe hits, or to wait until you find your religion. Or, you can find a piece of paper, think about what you want to achieve, write it down, and communicate it clearly with someone who can help you to achieve it. Get with it!

FOCUS MAKES IT POSSIBLE

On May 25, 1961, U.S. President John F. Kennedy delivered an address to a joint session of the U.S. Congress. He titled it "Urgent National Needs" and in it he made a breathtaking announcement: The United States would put a man on the moon and return him safely before the decade was out. Nothing could have been made clearer. It was a bold national initiative. Many believed it was not possible. Yet within nine years, the dream became a reality.

— Robert

OBSERVING

When the eyes say one thing, and the tongue another, a
practical man relies on the language of the first.
— RALPH WALDO EMERSON

Observation might be called the search for visual and
auditory clues to your partner's non-verbal communication (often
referred to as NVC). In other words, observation is verifying what you
hear and feel. Some describe it as "listening with your eyes."

Non-verbal communication gives you clues that can reveal a wealth of
information about the other person. By observing NVC, you can improve
your intuitive ability as a communicator and you will find yourself
having new insights, gut feelings, and revelations. Great communicators
trust their intuition and instincts and use them regularly. Do the same.

Have you ever noticed that you never really notice something until you
become interested in it? How often have you said to yourself, "I never
saw that before"? You cannot see what you choose to ignore. Observation requires an open mind and an increased awareness. It can register
split-second, fleeting expressions, gestures, and clues.

Like Sherlock Holmes or Columbo, you must search for visual clues.
Do they match what is being said? If not, then as Hamlet said,

"Something is rotten in this state of Denmark." For instance:

— Has a subordinate ever promised you a report, but something told you it wasn't a realistic promise?
— Your supervisor said no layoffs would result from a recent takeover. Why did something not seem right?
— You are confronting your child about an incident at school. He tells you one thing, but his fidgeting tells you something else.

This is NVC in action.

Seeing is *not* believing . . . believing is seeing. Look for the connections that exist between what is said verbally and non-verbally.

You can train yourself to become a better observer by simply focusing your attention for ten to fifteen minutes a day. Watch, hear, and experience what is happening around you. Notice your feelings about what's going on. The most important thing to notice is change. What's different, what has changed?

Ask yourself what others might be feeling. Inner emotions are reflected externally through minute changes in body language, facial language, and physiological clues (see the sections in this book named after these types of NVC). Notice these changes and you'll become aware of the inner emotions of others. Use this information to help you understand what is happening at the moment.

One isolated observation is not significant. Several observations indicating the same thing, and strong intuition that something is going on, *are* significant. In this respect, non-verbal communication is much more influential than the spoken word.

When observing others

1. Look for behaviors, traits, patterns, and clues that you can use
2. Interpret the significance of what you have observed
3. Verify the accuracy of your interpretation by asking questions
4. Use the information

LISTEN WITH YOUR EYES

A recent magazine story noted that individuals who had suffered traumatic injuries or strokes were significantly more likely to detect lying than were unaffected groups of individuals. How? By observing facial gestures and body language.

The people with brain damage were unable to speak or understand complete sentences, so they relied on observation. The unaffected groups focused more on the words used and were fooled more often. What's the lesson? Become more observant. Listen more with your eyes than your ears.

— **Robert**

OBSERVING: WHAT TO LOOK FOR

The more you look, the more you see.
— PETER

It's easy to say, "be observant," but observant of what? Here's what to look for.

1. Appearance
2. State of mind
3. Environment
4. Sensory preference
5. Behavioral language
6. Body language and physiological clues
7. Emotion

You can find more on these aspects of non-verbal communication in their related sections.

There is a whole host of things that observation can tell you once you put it into practice. Some of the most important are detailed below.

1. DO THEY LIKE YOU? SIGNS THAT PEOPLE LIKE YOU INCLUDE
   - Smiles
   - Mirroring your posture, actions, and gestures
   - Good eye contact
   - Placing themselves close to you
   - Having an open posture (arms uncrossed)
   - Facing you directly and appearing at ease and relaxed

2. ARE THEY INTERESTED IN YOUR IDEAS? IF THEY ARE, THEY MAY
   - Lean forward and closer to you
   - Become more expressive and communicative
   - Lean backward and relax
   - Widen their eyes and dilate their pupils as interest in what you're saying increases
   - Open their hands, unbutton their jackets, stroke their chins, or tilt their heads
   - Appear critical when, in fact, they are seriously considering your information

3. ARE THEY DEFENSIVE, SUSPICIOUS, OR DISAGREEING WITH YOU? THEY WILL DEMONSTRATE AN OBVIOUS ABSENCE OF ANY OF THE SIGNS OF INTEREST LISTED ABOVE. THEY MAY
   - Give you sideways glances
   - Close their hands and keep their jackets on and buttoned
   - Keep arms or legs crossed
   - Close their body positions off
   - Lean or move away from you, often toward the door
   - Turn away from you and toward the door
   - Develop tension in their faces
   - Make hand gestures over their mouths as if to hide from you
   - Touch or slightly rub their noses

OBSERVING . . . WHAT?

The body doesn't lie.

You walk into your boss's office and cheerfully ask, "Got a minute?"

She replies, "Yeah, sure," but glances at her watch, fidgets with some papers, and seems rather distant.

Is this a good time to talk? Unless it's an emergency, it's unlikely. Her body language says she's preoccupied and feeling pressured with time constraints.

What to do? Comment on her body language and ask to meet later. She'll be more receptive and more likely to accommodate you. You might sound like this: "You look busy and what I want to discuss can wait. It's about the ABC proposal. I'll need about ten to fifteen minutes. Can I meet with you this afternoon — say 2 p.m.?

Listen with your eyes as well as your ears.

— **Robert**

ONE-WAY COMMUNICATION

The mind can only absorb what the body can endure.
— ROBERT

Think back to high school. The teacher lectured; you listened. Or did you? If you had listened to two or three lectures before this one, chances are your attention span had shortened considerably. This is a typical example of one-way communication, which ignores the listener and focuses on the speaker. You had no opportunity to share what you understood — or more accurately, misunderstood.

Typically, things at work are hectic and rushed. Imagine your boss in a hurry giving you instructions for a difficult assignment. Of course, he then asks, "Do you understand?" Your immediate reply? "Yes."

This is typical one-way communication. In it, the misunderstanding remains hidden until you try to complete the task and find you didn't really understand. It's like getting directions to go somewhere. They all make sense until you get into a strange area. Then you wish you had listened more actively.

Maybe you thought you understood. Maybe you were afraid to ask questions because you didn't want to appear dumb or incapable. Maybe he intimidated you. Whatever the reason, everyone's time is wasted by misunderstanding.

The goal of good communication is shared understanding. Ideally, both participants must be open and flexible, and *want* to understand each other. Two-way communication allows thoughts and feelings to be shared.

ONCE OVER EASY

It was my first day working at the harness track. I wanted to make a great first impression. My boss explained how to put the harness on the horse and fasten the cart to it. He asked me if I understood. I said I did. I was nervous and didn't want to appear ignorant.

I harnessed the horse, then pulled the cart up and told the boss his horse was ready. He jumped into the cart and the cart flipped over. I had forgotten to tie the cart to the harness.

The moral? Avoid one-way communication in giving instructions.

1. Explain.
2. Demonstrate.
3. Ask questions of your listener.
4. Watch him or her do it the first time.

— **Robert**

OPEN QUESTIONS

Children ask better questions than do adults. "May I have a cookie?" "Why is the sky blue?" and "What does a cow say?" are far more likely to elicit a cheerful response than "Where's your manuscript?" "Why haven't you called?" and "Who's your lawyer?"
— FRAN LEBOWITZ

When you ask a question, the listener must get in touch with and interpret her feelings and ideas. It takes time for the listener to access this information and to put her answers into words. Then, you acknowledge that you understand the answers and continue through the cycle of questions.

The most important part of any question is the response it evokes. You should be aware of the differences between two different types of questions: closed questions and open questions (see also *Closed Questions*).

Open questions don't permit a simple "yes" or "no" answer, and you can't control the direction of the conversation with them. You can, however, use them to draw someone out and get his opinion.

These types of questions can implant ideas and indirectly guide the listener's thoughts. They tap directly into the listener's thoughts and feelings. They stimulate self-discovery and seek to discover pleasures and pains. Open questions encourage dialogue by asking for elaboration on an idea, and they can stimulate spontaneity and creativity.

PROBE DEEPLY FOR DISCOVERY

Open questions often start with "who," "what," "when," "where," "why," and "how."

Open questions strive for thoughts, feelings, and opinions, not facts. This comes more from your intent in asking the question. While they might be answered with short answers, they tend to go deeper and reveal something about the person who is answering. If they are used effectively, they can't be answered with a simple "yes" or "no," since they encourage elaboration and promote self-discovery.

"Who will be there? Who should be there? Who else?"

"Why do you think these changes are necessary? Why would we want to wait? Why could we improve the process?"

"What do you feel are the most important steps in the process? What would it take to get you to agree? What do you think of the cosmetic changes?"

"Where could we improve our service? Where do you anticipate problems? Where would you suggest we go?"

"When are the best times to call? When do you think you'll be ready to move forward with these plans? When do you foresee these changes occurring?"

"How could we improve this? How will it work for you? How can we better meet our customer's needs?"

Initially, try to avoid asking "why" questions. They may evoke a simple "because" response, with no further dialogue to follow. They can also be perceived as threatening and condescending. "Why wasn't that project finished on time?" or "Why are we always waiting for you?" sounds accusatory and condescending.

"How," "what," and "is there" questions are the best types of questions to use. "How would you feel if you were held up because someone didn't complete their project on time?" asks the same question as "Why wasn't that project finished on time?" but without the threatening tone of "why." Consider also how inclusive and friendly these questions sound: "What would you have done in that situation?" "Is there anything else you would do to improve performance?"

If you want to go on a voyage of true discovery, implant ideas, broaden the topic, or learn someone's inner thoughts and feelings, ask open questions.

ASK OPEN QUESTIONS TO IMPROVE UNDERSTANDING

Beware of the person who knows the answer before he understands the question.

George exclaimed, "Yeah, I'll have that account sewn up before tomorrow. No problem."

I asked, "Sewn up — how? What steps are you going to take to reach an agreement?"

As George stammered to answer, it became apparent that he had no clear plan to close the account. By asking him pertinent open questions, I was able to sit down with him and discuss an appropriate strategy. I didn't argue. I didn't assume he didn't have a plan. I led him to discover that for himself, by allowing him to express his ideas out loud.

Open questions stimulate deeper responses and often point you in the direction of improved understanding — yours and theirs.

— Robert

PARTNERS

Conversation is like a dear little baby that is brought in to be handed around. You must rock it, nurse it, keep it on the move if you want to keep it smiling.
— KATHERINE MANSFIELD

The "right" conversational partner is an important part of getting what you want. Knowing what you want helps you determine who you need to talk to. Too often, we waste too much time talking to the wrong person. In conversation, focus your energy on finding out who can help you get what you want. Then, concentrate on ways to get along with, or connect with, that person. Connecting is often referred to as "rapport." We prefer the term "connecting," however, since it implies an active process dependent on you.

TELL THEM ABOUT IT

It's human nature to complain to everyone except the person who can do something about the problem.

Have you noticed how most people want you to sympathize with their problems? They don't want you to question how they contributed to the problem, or to ask them what they plan to do about it. That's too threatening for them. They just want you to feel sorry for them.

I remember complaining to anyone who would listen about how useless it was to study Latin. This covered up for my lack of study and justified my poor grades. If only I had gone to my Latin teacher and confessed my problem. Instead, I failed and had to repeat Latin in summer school. Oh well — Helen had to repeat Latin as well. I remember telling all my friends how pretty I thought Helen was. Now that I look back on those days, I wish I had told her.

Connect with and tell the people who can help you about your situation. You'll be glad you did.

— **Robert**

| PEERS

It's a fallacy to think you have to like everyone you work with, yet you do have to work with them.
— ROBERT

Getting along with those you have no immediate authority over (or they over you) can be a rocky road. Smooth out the bumps by following these guidelines.

1. **Clarify areas of responsibility, authority, and overlap.** How much authority do you have? What specifically are you responsible for? Is the responsibility or authority to make decisions shared with anyone else?
2. **Identify and separate available resources.** Who else is going to help you? What's the budget? What's the time frame?
3. **Negotiate conflicts.** You have no clear authority over your peers, so you need to negotiate a resolution when conflicts arise. Think win/win.
4. **Offer feedback and help.** Keep other interested parties informed as to your progress. When others are waiting on you, ask for their help to improve the process. When they lag behind, offer suggestions to help them.

5. **Network outside your department.** By keeping a solid network of contacts outside your department, you will be in the know. You'll have someone to go to for favors. Networking is the way to greater cooperation and less stress at work.

YOU MEET PEERS EVERYWHERE

When I was a salesman, I used to work with a colleague who I considered to be not too bright. We both labored together for a time, then he decided to go his own way. I was not displeased. Several years later I called on a company to sell them a system, and — lo and behold — my old sales colleague was the vice president of the company. Suddenly he seemed much more intelligent than I had ever given him credit for.

Your peers can turn up in the strangest places. Try to never burn your bridges with comments or actions you can't take back!

— Peter

PERCEPTION

"I see nobody on the road," said Alice.
"I only wish I had such eyes," the King remarked in a
fretful tone. "To be able to see Nobody! And at that
distance, too!
Why, it's as much as I can do to see real people, by this
light!" — LEWIS CARROLL

If you ever have the opportunity to scuba dive, you'll be amazed to find you can't see any of the magnificent underwater colors of the deep coral reefs without a light. Colors are filtered out in water. The deeper you go, the more filtered the color becomes. Yet with a portable light, you can appreciate them in all their magnificence.

Your perceptions, like water, filter facts — and those filtered facts become your reality. In fact, your version of reality is *fiercely* protected by your personal beliefs. The messages you receive from others are run through these perceptual filters, and the filters distort the messages. Messages that are full of distorted facts and generalizations become fertile ground for communication roadblocks.

Once you become aware of your perceptual filters, you can appreciate how they affect your communications. And there are infinite perceptions of reality, because each of us has our own unique perceptions.

Yet you can shed light on your reality (like shining a light underwater to restore the colored beauty of coral reefs) by widening your perceptual filters. You can, in fact, change your reality by perceiving it differently. To do this, listen carefully, observe, and question — so you can eliminate your biases and become more flexible and accepting of differences. Education's purpose is to open your mind with possibilities, not close it with prejudice.

WHAT IS THE TRUTH?

Do you watch *The X-Files?* Is the truth really out there? Most of us only want to know the truth if it supports our views.

I've noticed that regardless of all of the facts, we focus on those that support our view of reality. Then we say, "See, I told you so," or "Just as I suspected." This observation prompted Shakespeare to say, "There is no such thing as good or bad, right or wrong, but thinking makes it so."

My point is this: It's difficult, if not impossible, to be fully open-minded. Try listening to the other person as if you were that person in that situation. Then evaluate the evidence.

— Robert

| PERSUADING

If you would convince others, seem open to convincing yourself.
— LORD CHESTERFIELD

Your persuasive ability can be enhanced by the creative use of body language. Become a whole-body communicator. Here are five key approaches:

1. BE NATURAL AND SPONTANEOUS

   Remember to breathe deeply. This will re-oxygenate your mind and body. Don't try to be someone you are not. Be you. Be present. Be involved. Speak with your eyes. Remember Leonardo da Vinci: The eyes are the windows of the soul. Expose your soul and you will capture the heart of your listener.

2. AVOID DISTRACTING MANNERISMS

   Verbal fillers, such as "um's," "ah's," and the ever-present "Canajun eh's" are distracting. Don't fidget or play with things. Remove obstacles that prevent connection to your listener.

3. EXPRESS YOUR EMOTIONS

Be excited and passionate. Let your excitement be reflected in your face. A poker face may help in poker, but it doesn't foster open communication.

4. ARTICULATE WHAT YOU HEAR, SEE, AND FEEL BEFORE YOU ARTICULATE WHAT YOU WANT

Be able to articulate what the listener wants and how he or she feels. Display the ability to share the emotions and feelings of this person.

5. LET YOUR LISTENER BE YOUR MIRROR

Look for signs of acceptance in your partner's response and action. Your partner will tell you what direction you need to go next.

IMAGINING CAN GET YOU THERE!

Create a peak state. A peak state prepares you to be successful.

You need to first persuade yourself before you can persuade anyone else — take a lesson from some of the great actors.

Great actors persuade us they are who they portray themselves to be. They first persuade themselves mentally and physically. Through visualization and imagination, they imagine themselves to be other people, feeling what those people would feel. They physically get into the body positions and contort their faces into the features that create those emotions they wish to portray. And thus, each actor virtually becomes another person.

What's the point? Imagine yourself being successful and full of confidence. Stand tall. Walk proud. Smile. It will release endorphins that will make you feel better. Endorphins don't work as well as Prozac — but they'll help.

— **Robert**

PHYSIOLOGICAL CLUES

A man finds room in the few square inches of his face for the traits of all his ancestors; for the expression of all his history, and his wants.
— RALPH WALDO EMERSON

Physiological, or physical, changes are often so subtle they're easily missed. They're not gross changes in facial expressions (which are readily seen). Rather, they are very subtle, or "fine," changes in the components that make up the face (skin, muscles, mouth, eyes, etc.). Changes in a person's physiology are usually significant. Remember that no one isolated gesture can be considered significant, but *clusters of gestures* indicating the same thing are important. What kinds of physiological changes can you notice?

1. **Skin and color changes.** Look for a flush in the cheeks, or perhaps a blanching of the skin color.
2. **Muscle twitches,** especially in the small muscles of the face, and particularly around the eyes and mouth. Such changes don't have a single universal meaning, but are habitual in any one person. Any change in their normal pattern is significant.
3. **Breathing patterns** may change. (You can see the rate of breathing by

watching the shoulders move.) Watch shoulders rise with inhalation and drop with exhalation. That's the most consistent way to detect increases or decreases in breathing rate. Breathing is an unconscious physical response. It differs from person to person, but is consistent within the individual. As thought processes change, so does the breathing pattern. If we get excited or stressed, our breathing pattern increases. If we're relaxed and comfortable, it slows down.

4. **Smiles** are important, and we can detect them from quite a distance. They are disarming and seductive, and even though they're universally recognized as a sign of happiness, even a smile can carry mixed messages. Smiles can be
   - Playful
   - Seductive
   - Shy
   - Welcoming
   - Tolerant
   - Condescending and insincere
   - Warm, sincere, and friendly
   - Polite
   - Social

5. **Eye adjustments.** Watch the pupil (the black circle within the colored iris) for size changes. The pupil can dilate or constrict.
   - It will dilate when the person is involved in an intimate conversation, or if the person is deeply involved and focused on a general conversation.
   - It will constrict as a person mentally "wanders" or is thinking about something else.

REMEMBER WHEN?

I remember looking into her eyes (I'm asking for trouble if I say her name). They were wide open and longing. She gazed at me with her pupils widely dilated. There was a slight tremor in her voice. Her cheeks were flushed and her breathing was rapid. I knew the moment was right, so I pressed her close to me and kissed her. It was passionate, prolonged, and sweet. Her wonderful response proved that those sweet little telltale signs said so much more than words could ever hope to.

— **Robert**

POSITIVE RESULTS

You gotta accentuate the positive, eliminate the
negative . . .
— JOHNNY MERCER

A few things in life are guaranteed: taxes, death, and problems. You'll get your share of negatives. But you can deal with them when you have to. Here's how.

1. **Single one out.** Find the negative thought, idea, behavior, or comment that is bothering you most. Isolate it and describe it. Be specific.
2. **Get knowledge.** Learn all you can about how to do it. Read books. Listen to tapes. Find a mentor.
3. **Turn it around.** Change your thinking to change your behavior. Take your negative and reverse it into a positive. Pretend you can do what you don't think you can do. Imagine that you can't fail. In your mind, turn that negative thought, idea, behavior, or comment into success.
4. **Act as if you can't fail.** Act means to do. Go ahead and just do it. Do the best you can. Be aware of your results and adjust them if you don't get the results you're after.
5. **Ask yourself, "What did I learn?"** Keep a log. Record your results. Plan

how you'll do it better next time.

6. **Create a positive story about it.** Remember that the number of people who will attend your funeral will be affected more by the weather than anything you will ever do in your lifetime. Don't take yourself so seriously. Laugh at yourself and the world will laugh with you, not at you.

AN ACCENT: POSITIVE OR NEGATIVE?

Reading this book, you cannot hear that I have an accent, but I do. When I give keynotes, I always ask my audience, "Do you notice I have an accent?" They laugh, and then I explain that I can speak fluent English like them. I also explain, "I kept my Swiss accent so you have to listen more carefully" — which is absolutely not true. I kept it because I couldn't get rid of it, and my audience knows it . . . it makes them all part of the game.

— Peter

PRESENTING

The worst human fears:
Speaking in front of an audience
Dying
Speaking and dying in front of an audience.
— PETER

Speaking to your communication partner or another individual, one-on-one, is what this book is all about. But even if you're addressing only one person, you're "presenting," and the principles that make for a good presentation to large groups will apply.

So, to give the right impression, you might want to brush up on your presentation skills — because there are a lot more factors to consider when you present to an audience. There are five quintessential elements to a powerful presentation:

1. The speech itself
2. Your body language
3. The equipment you need to do it properly
4. The environment in which you are speaking
5. The necessary preparation

In a sense, these elements mirror the kinds of things you need to consider when talking to your partner:

1. Your words
2. Your partner's body language, as well as your own
3. Special equipment or props, if you need them
4. Your environment
5. Your self-preparation

To speak one-on-one is what this book is all about. For more information on how to speak with more power to groups, you should study *Secrets of Power Presentations* by Peter Urs Bender (see *Recommended Reading*).

PREPARATION IS THE KEY

Five hundred people!

My first presentation was at a scientific conference in front of five hundred people. I had dual slide projectors, two remote controls, and a handheld microphone. The room was dark and I had no way to point to slides. I used my finger to point — which was completely useless in a dark room. I mixed up the remotes and got out of sequence with my slides. I dropped the microphone. I felt like a complete idiot.

My point? Whether you speak to one person or five hundred, you're presenting. Know your purpose, prepare, have a plan, practice, and before you start, read *Secrets of Power Presentations*.

— Robert

PROCRASTINATORS

It is an undoubted truth, that the less one has to do, the less time one finds to do it in. One yawns, one procrastinates, one can do it when one will, and therefore one seldom does it at all.
— LORD CHESTERFIELD

Next to saying "no," overcoming procrastination is the best time-management tool I've found. But overcoming it is difficult in ourselves and downright frustrating when we work with procrastinators.

We procrastinate for different reasons:

— Expressives — because the job might not be high-profile enough
— Drivers — because it's not a high priority to them
— Amiables — because there is too much dissension
— Analyticals — because they're afraid of being wrong

I've discovered that people need either structure or support to overcome procrastination. Structure is the "know-how" to be successful. Support is the ongoing encouragement, inspiration, and reassurance they need to apply the know-how. Find out which is missing, provide it, and cope using the following steps.

How to work with procrastinators:

— Surface their fears and make it safe to be honest

— Help them to solve problems, prioritize, and make decisions

— Stress your dependence on them, as well as the importance of the project

— Build mutual trust by supporting their decisions

— Reassure them regularly

KEEP AFTER PROCRASTINATION

It's easier to get others to agree to do better next time than to get them to do better today. This sad but true reality makes itself apparent every time we give someone feedback. I once had to correct an employee's behavior (excessive and prolonged breaks). Of course, each time I confronted the issue, he had a good reason but assured me it wouldn't happen again. Eventually I explained the consequences (dismissal) in a direct manner. I followed up faithfully and let him know I wasn't going to leave this issue alone. He changed.

— Robert

QUESTIONS

No question is so difficult to answer as the one to which the answer is obvious.
— George Bernard Shaw

Questions are powerful and underused. Questions control the direction and content of a conversation, and the person who asks the questions is in control. Questions help establish a common topic of interest and then zero in on that topic. Questions may change someone's beliefs, behaviors, or level of awareness.

Questions are the window to the mind. The trick is to know what questions to ask, how and when to ask them — and sometimes even whom to ask.

Questions are used to gather information, and avoid misunderstandings and mistakes. They can be used to

— Plant the seeds of ideas
— Start conversations
— Build rapport
— Establish trust
— Ensure understanding

- Motivate people
- Solve problems
- Gain cooperation
- Overcome objections and hostility

Ask questions to

- Learn what is important to the listener
- Influence decisions
- Gain information
- Guide the listener's thinking and actions

Here are five excellent reasons to ask a question.

1. **To draw attention to yourself or an important issue.** For instance, "Hi, how are you? May I _____? Could you help me? Did you notice the _____? What do you think of the _____ ?"
2. **To gather information.** Remember the Reporter's Creed — five W's and an H — who, what, when, where, why, and how.
3. **To give information.** "In this situation would you consider _____? What is there left to do? What would you think of _____ ?"
4. **To plant an idea.** "Have you ever wondered if _____? Are you ready to consider _____?"
5. **To signal the end.** "Isn't it time to 'get off the pot'? What are we waiting for?"

Penetrating questions force you and your partner to go inward and search for new discoveries. They're like peeling the layers off an onion. The deeper you go, the closer to the core you come. Old ways of thinking and seeing are in the superficial layers. New perspectives and insights emerge as you move closer to the core.

Thought-provoking questions can be stressful. They force you to expand your realities and worldviews. You begin to question your actions when faced with them. This is a healthy situation. It's how you continue to grow and develop. It also deepens your relationship with the person asking you the questions.

To guide someone's thinking, plant the seed of an idea and help it germinate by asking questions. Ask, "Which proposal do you prefer?" Or ask, "How does what I'm saying compare with what you're already doing?" People will consider your ideas when you ask them thoughtful questions.

To start a conversation, build rapport, and establish trust, say, "Hi, my name's Sandy. What's yours?" Or "Hi! How are you?" Or "What's your opinion on ———?" Or ask such questions as "How do you feel about ——————— ? How can I help you with ——————— ? Could you tell me about ——————— ?"

To ensure you understand the message, ask, "Then I understand you to mean . . . ?" Or say, "That's an interesting point of view. What makes you say that?"

To motivate, try turning a question around when someone asks you one. For instance, if you're asked, "What is the purpose of doing it that way?" reply, "What do *you* think is the purpose of doing it that way?" Force the questioner to evaluate the importance of the question. Find out what's important to him or her. Search for hidden pains or pleasures by asking questions. Persuasive people link benefits important to their listeners with benefits associated with their proposals.

To solve problems, ask "what-if" questions. "If not this, then what?" Or "What if we had no other choice? How would we cope? What can you suggest?"

To gain cooperation and overcome objections and hostility, ask directly, "What are your concerns?" Restate the objections as though you don't quite understand, then be silent. Wait for your partner to elaborate. Ask bluntly, "What would it take to come together on this?" Take notice of what is important. Answer the objections as best you can and conclude with, "If I do this, would you still be concerned?"

Remember that any time you approach someone with questions, they will tend to feel defensive and stressed. Begin tactfully by acknowledging the person's emotional state. Conclude your conversation by asking, "Is there anything else I should know that I haven't asked?" You may have missed something that your partner considers important.

Finally, to avoid misunderstandings, mistakes, and wasted time or money, ask, "Do you understand? Can you help me understand?" Expressing such thoughts and concerns helps both of you to clarify and organize your thoughts.

The principle is to go from the general to the specific — this is what we call the *floodlight/spotlight* approach. One good approach is to pretend you're a journalist trying to get a story. Start by asking universal, general, open questions to discover what gives this person pleasure or pain. Listen for hot buttons (key words and phrases), as well as the benefits the person considers important. Discover the person's strengths and weaknesses. Shine a floodlight on your partner. Make your communication partner the star.

For example: "Tell me about _____ . How do you feel about _____? What is your position on _____?" These questions demonstrate your interest. Your partner feels acknowledged and will usually answer freely.

If you have established and maintained rapport during the discovery phase by asking general, open questions, you may now take control of the conversation by using specific, closed questions. Open questions help you isolate objections (threats to success) as well as identify needs and common ground (opportunities for success). Closed questions will help you get specific information and guide thinking.

Start by acknowledging common ground. When you say it, your partner will doubt you. When your partner says it, it must be true!

Let's say you're discussing the company's computer system and you both agree it's outdated. Your listener feels that the expense of a new system can't be justified.

Here's how it might go:

"Do you agree the system is outdated?" (General point of agreement.)

"Is the cost your only objection?" (His objection. If his answer is "yes," then . . .)

"If I could show you how the initial investment would pay for itself many times over, would you be interested in replacing the system?"

Try to phrase the question to get a "yes" response. Don't give your partner the option of responding with a "no." Asking for a "yes" answer is more positive and will set a trend in the conversation. Now address your partner's concern using a technique such as the *feel/felt/found* approach (see *Answers*).

Here's how it works: "I know how you *feel*. I *felt* exactly the same way when I started looking at the system. What I *found* was that replacing it would increase productivity tenfold. My point is that it will cost a bit to replace the system, but the benefit is vastly increased productivity."

Now change the spotlight back to a floodlight. Go from the specific to the general to enlist support. Ask, "If we were to commit to a new system, what else do you suggest we consider?" Once your partner starts to offer suggestions, he or she is starting to think favorably about your proposal. That's the beginning of support.

ALWAYS ASK QUESTIONS

It seems that most employees are always searching for impending changes in the workplace so they can question them. You can employ the same strategy to uncover their concerns.

Once, a negative employee who was disgruntled with shift changes confronted me. He wanted me to justify the change. I asked him which change or changes in particular created the problem for him. I got the typical, "Well, we've always done it this way — who do you think you are?" response.

I acknowledged his response and asked if there was anything else bothering him. He said no. I then asked if he was prepared to quit over the change, to which he said no. I then explained the reason for the change and asked if he would help me explain it to the others. To my surprise, he agreed.

When in doubt, ask questions.

— Robert

REFLECTING

The essence of being human is that
one does not seek perfection.
— GEORGE ORWELL

Feedback is an important part of the *HEART* approach to active listening. The "R" in *HEART* stands for *Reflect and paraphrase* — reflect for your partner's sake and paraphrase for yours. The advantage of reflective listening is the opportunity it creates for the speaker to clear up misunderstandings. You pause, rephrase in your own words, then ask your partner to confirm your understanding. Reflect on feelings, content, and behavior.

Reflect feelings? Yes! When feelings interfere with the progress of your communication — if your partner acts indifferent to you — it's important to identify what he or she is feeling. Are the feelings positive, negative, or indifferent? Is your partner angry, frustrated, excited, preoccupied? You need to know how feelings are affecting the conversation.

Reflect on the content of your communication by paraphrasing what your partner has said, using *your partner's* key words. Try to capture the essence of what was said. If the message was complicated, try summarizing the comments to ensure you understand the gist of the message.

Reflect on your partner's behavior — without judging it. If your partner is exhibiting actions you don't understand (e.g., eye-rolling, questioning tone of voice) ask what is meant by the behavior. If you get the feeling she's saying one thing but thinking another, reflect on that. Reflect what you see, hear, and feel, but don't interpret it. Describe it to her, and try to get her to explain it to you. Reflect to verify, clarify, and summarize. Focus on the intended meaning of the message *and* the feelings behind it. Make sure what you thought she said is, in fact, what she meant.

Don't try to manipulate your partner's words when you reflect. Attempt to improve your understanding. Tap into her insights.

Use phrases such as, "What I hear you saying is this:_____. Is that correct?" Always conclude by asking, "Am I missing anything? Do I have the gist of what you're saying? Do you feel I've heard you correctly?" This helps the speaker know that you do (or don't) understand. It also gives the person the opportunity to explain until you *do* understand. But a note of caution here: If you reflect and paraphrase everything, you will annoy most speakers. Use your discretion. Only reflect and paraphrase key information that you feel you don't understand.

THE ART OF REFLECTING

Be sure to judge yourself before you judge others.

Once during a conversation, someone said, "I missed the point." I replied, "Missed the point?" She then went into greater detail to ensure I understood her confusion. Reflecting is an art. Don't overdo it, don't make it obvious, and above all remember: Less is more and being subtle is better than being obvious.

— Robert

RESPONSES

No response is still a response.
— ROBERT

Responses are based on one or more of four different things: perceptions, experiences, interpretations, or generalizations. They can tell you a lot about the person who is being questioned.

1. *Perceptions* are based on what you deem *significant at that moment.* If, for instance, you witnessed an auto accident with a teenage driver, your focus would likely be on the teenager, and your response to the question "What happened?" would likely reflect that focus. You would *perceive* that the most significant element of the accident was the teenage driver.

2. *Experiences* are based on your past. If you're asked, "Have you witnessed a similar accident before?" you might reply, "Yes, and the teen was speeding in that situation as well." You might also have read recently about several incidents in which teens were caught speeding. These situations might influence your present response.

3. *Interpretations* involve combining your perceptions with your

experiences. If you're asked, "What do you think the cause of the accident was?" you might state that the driver was a teen, and that the speed the teen was going was the cause of the accident.

4. *Generalizations* state your beliefs. If you're asked, "Have you noticed any similarities between this and the other accident you saw?" you might generalize that most teen accidents are a result of speeding, and that teens should not be allowed to drive.

Each level of response takes you into a deeper level of understanding. You can learn more about the other person and how he or she perceives the world. You may not agree, but you understand where the person is coming from and why he or she is responding in this way.

RESPONSES ARE A REALITY CHECK ON BELIEFS

While on a break during a seminar in Texas, a participant stated that he had no problem with blacks and whites being in the same schools or being friends, but he didn't like interracial relationships (interpretation). I was already wishing I was somewhere else.

He went on to say he had noticed an increase in interracial relationships in his area (perception) and he had been raised to keep to his own (experience). When I asked him what his objections were, he could only say, "Well, we're different — you know, different cultures and beliefs and so on. They could never work (generalizations)."

I replied, "So are you and I — different, that is."

My point? If nothing else, someone's response will tell how firmly entrenched his or her beliefs are.

— **Robert**

RHYTHM

How can you tell the dancer from the dance?
— William Butler Yeats

Throughout time, rhythm has united people. It continues to unite us today. It is probably true to say that rhythm is a language in itself, one that transcends all other languages. You do not need to know a language in order to be moved by the rhythms inherent in it. How often have you seen pictures of tourists from Western nations dancing with native people in Africa? They're not faking it. They're genuinely moved by the rhythms they are encountering — perhaps for the first time.

How much more powerful, then, is rhythm coupled with language? There is a rhythm to all communication, and it's established through gestures, body language, facial expressions, rate of speech, and vocal qualities.

When our movements, actions, and words easily, fully, and completely fall into sync with someone else's, we establish a strong connection with that person. Even human silence is easy and comfortable when people are in sync with each other. Getting into sync involves using the matching techniques we have described elsewhere in this book (see *Matching*). Some come to us naturally. Others require a little conscious practice.

DANCING ISN'T MY FORTE

Let me say at the outset that I am not a dancer . . . I dance by numbers. Although dances are often learned that way initially, it's difficult for someone with an accounting mindset to escape the invariability of the "system." Only once in my life did I ever become uninhibited enough to "let go" and become one with the dance. I was in a conga line at a South American resort, and became one with the other dancers in that line — perhaps because I could see they were as inexperienced as I was. Whatever the case, it wasn't until the dance was over that I realized I had no idea what I had done, and no recollection of having danced to the numbers. That's what real rhythm can do for you.

— Peter

ROADBLOCKS

We all face roadblocks, but those who ask for
help frequently avoid them.
— PETER

Have you ever been in a hurry to drive somewhere and traffic was at a standstill? It's for good reason that we call such traffic "gridlock." It makes you feel frustrated and helpless. The question "Why me?" comes immediately to mind, along with "How do I get out of this? What else can I do? Which exit will get me clear?"

Communication roadblocks are just as frustrating. You may know exactly where you want to go, what you want to say, and what you want to do . . . but roadblocks stop you by distorting your intended meaning. Effective communication can occur only when the message that is received is exactly the same as the message that was sent.

Roadblocks can be personal or interpersonal.

Personal roadblocks include

— Fear of failure
— Lack of confidence
— Worry

- Depression
- Indifference
- Distortions
- Frustrations
- Dislikes
- Preoccupations
- Lack of knowledge
- Poor communication skills
- Faulty assumptions
- Strong emotional involvement
- Personal or physical distractions
- Suspicion
- Poor listening skills

Interpersonal roadblocks include

- Different thought processes
- Stereotyping
- Prejudice
- Disagreement
- Lack of authority or self-esteem
- Lack of trust or credibility
- Social conflict
- Political or cultural differences
- Poor communication skills
- Different values, beliefs, or attitudes
- Competition and power struggles
- Disregard for the importance of relationships

Communication patterns also vary between genders, cultures, industries, occupations, generations, countries, and educational backgrounds. All these present communication roadblocks. They twist, obscure, and distort the intended message. Your goal is to become aware of these barriers and maneuver around them.

In general, there are five main causes of roadblocks. They are:

1. Sensory differences
2. Motivational differences
3. Time differences
4. Perceptual differences
5. Assumptions

See the sections dealing with these topics for more.

ROADBLOCKS: OTHERS OFTEN SEE THEM MORE CLEARLY

If someone can see both sides of the problem, then it's likely he doesn't have his money invested in it. Yet I'm always amazed by how someone can walk in on a conversation, listen in, and offer a suggestion that fits. Why? The person is not emotionally involved. She or he has fewer roadblocks to contend with.

Keep it simple. Control your emotions. Don't judge. It's tough but it's necessary.

— Robert

SAYING "NO"

Sometimes "no" is a complete sentence.
— ROBERT

Saying "no" tactfully yet effectively can present a problem, but it's your best time-management tool. It takes confidence, and how you say it is more important than what you say. Make sure you are definitive and have a downward inflection in your voice to sound emphatic.

The following are ways to cushion the blow of the "no."

— Ask for time to think about it. "Can I get back to you tomorrow on that?"
— Renegotiate terms you can agree to saying "yes" to. "I can't contribute $50 but I'd be happy to contribute $10."
— Say "no" and offer an alternative. "No, I can't help, but you might ask me next month when I have more time."
— Say "no" as a complete sentence. "NO." This works best when someone is being persistent and won't take no for an answer.
— Ask for something in return, and if they say "no" you have restored balance. "I would love to help you if you would . . . "

— Say "yes," but explain all you have to accomplish and ask them to decide which tasks you shouldn't do. "Yes, I would like to do it. But in order to do it, I'll have to not do this or this. Which do you suggest I eliminate?" This works well when you're saying no to your boss.

— Say "no, because . . . " This offers an explanation. "No, unfortunately I can't, because . . . "

WHAT'S THE MISSING INGREDIENT?

How you say "no" matters more than what you say.

Often, when people give you their favorite recipe, they forget to include a small but important ingredient or detail. Why? So yours doesn't taste quite as good as theirs, of course. I know many people have trouble saying "no," Amiables and Expressives in particular. I've watched them hem and haw and fidget. In order for your "no" to work, your body language and vocal tone must *mean* "no." That's the missing ingredient. Don't say I left it out.

— Robert

SENSES

There is no way in which to understand the world without first detecting it through the radar-net of our senses.
— DIANE ACKERMAN

We perceive things differently. As we detail in *Sensory Preference,* we relate to the world through our eyes (visual), ears (auditory), feelings (kinesthetic), sense of smell (olfactory), and taste (gustatory). Gustatory and olfactory senses don't play a major role in communication (at least in North America). But though each of us can use all our senses, each of us has a preference for — and selectively uses — only one or two. Good listeners listen for the appropriate sensory words from our partners and learn to react to them.

For instance: Imagine you are a visual person and your subordinate is kinesthetic. You are animated, speak quickly, and use visual terms. He speaks very slowly and takes long pauses to imagine how it would "feel" to do what is required. He comes to you for assistance.

"Excuse me, there's a problem . . . "

"Yes?"

"Well . . . (long pause) . . . I can't *get a handle on* . . . (long pause) . . . well, the new phone system."

"Look, the rep *showed* you how to use the system. Weren't you *watching*? I can't *see* what the problem is," you say, getting irritated at how long this is taking.

Your subordinate, now feeling rushed and unheard, answers, "Well . . . (long pause) I'll just *try* to use it and learn as I go."

A better way to handle this roadblock would have been to listen to how the person communicated. As a visual communicator you could have slowed down, acknowledged his frustration in kinesthetic terms, and helped him to find what was missing so that he could "feel" better about it.

WATCH HOW YOU TREAT YOUR HORSE

This was vividly driven home for me in my former life as a veterinarian, when I *showed* (visual) a client how to care for a horse with a wound on its chest. I wanted to leave it open and allow it to drain and close.

I asked her if she could *see* (visual) why it was important to leave it open and keep it clean. She said she didn't *feel* good (kinesthetic) about not bandaging it. I replied I had *seen* (visual) many of these types of wounds and leaving it unbandaged was fine. She still *felt* uncomfortable (kinesthetic).

I changed my tack. I then suggested she might *feel* uncomfortable (kinesthetic) about it but she should *try* it (kinesthetic). Sometimes it's difficult to *grasp* (kinesthetic) a concept that is new for us.

She then agreed to leave it open and *cleanse* it (kinesthetic) three times a day.

— Robert

SENSORY PREFERENCE

Seeing, hearing, feeling . . . these are the sentinels of our sensory life and shape the character of the people we become.
— PETER

In order to connect with confidence, you must determine if your listener's sensory preference is visual, auditory, or kinesthetic (see *Sensory Words*). This involves more than just the words someone chooses. What else does it involve?

— Gestures
— Rate of speech
— Eye movements
— How your partner moves

You will quickly notice the following characteristics:

1. *Visual people* are fast-moving and fast-talking. They breathe shallowly and use large, animated gestures. They tend to look up as they speak.
2. *Auditory people* are slower-talking, more rhythmic, slower-breathing,

and less animated in their gestures. They tend to look straight ahead as they speak.

3. *Kinesthetic people* are very slow-moving and slow-speaking and they use few or no gestures. They breathe very deeply. Their speech is very deliberate and they tend to look down when they speak.

SWING FOR THE BLEACHERS

The difference between speaking to someone's preferred sense and just speaking to the senses is like the difference between hitting a single and hitting a home run. If you speak to an individual's preferred sense, you will find that less time is required for the person to understand your point. You will connect more readily and you will be more persuasive.

I had trouble when I first started to apply these principles. I found that simply being aware of any difference was significant. Did he speak faster or slower, was he more or less animated, did he speak softer or louder? These were all valid differences. Rather than being annoyed by them, I adopted them into that specific conversation.

— **Robert**

SENSORY WORDS

You may choose your word like a connoisseur,
And polish it up with art,
But the word that sways, and stirs, and stays,
Is the word that comes from the heart.
— ELLA WHEELER WILCOX

We all assume that everyone else sees the world the same way we do, hears things the same way we hear them, and feels about things the same way we do. Nothing could be further from the truth. Each of us receives, processes, and remembers information differently. Our perceptions of reality are not reality — they are how we *believe* reality to be. This is why witnesses recall details differently in a trial, and why we think we're right and others are wrong.

In fact, the first sentence of the paragraph above gives us the clue to the three types of sensory preference words:

1. Visual words
2. Auditory words
3. Kinesthetic (emotional) words

We learn by using our eyes, ears, and feelings (touch and emotional sensations). This visual, auditory, and kinesthetic information is stored in the same form as it is received — as images, sounds, emotions, or feelings. Knowing this in advance reduces the time it takes to be understood.

We think and speak using words that come from our preferred senses. We also remember using these sensory words.

1. If we store information visually, we use visual words to describe the pictures in our minds.
2. If we store information as sounds, we use auditory words and phrases to describe those sounds.
3. If we store information as feelings and emotions, we use kinesthetic words and phrases to describe these feelings and emotions.

While each of us has the ability to use all three senses to store and describe information, most of us prefer using predominantly two of these methods. If you communicate with me using words that speak to a sense other than my preferred sense, I filter, alter, and distort your message much more than if I receive it in my preferred mode. The point? Use words that speak to your partner's preferred sense so that he or she may better understand you.

For example: Your partner has a preference for visual communication. Your sense of the world is auditory. If your partner doesn't understand what you're saying, use visual terms such as "picture this," "the way I see it," or "look at it this way." The choice of words is important in helping your partner "get the picture."

Knowing that communication proceeds on visual, auditory, and kinesthetic (or emotional) levels, how would you talk to a group? To get your message across, you would try to mix visual, auditory, and kinesthetic words into your speech. Replace the phrase "in other words . . . " with "you would likely see . . . " or "what it sounds like is . . . " or "you might feel like . . . " You would not just repeat your point. You would actually use other words. For example:

I knew it was a robin because I saw its red breast, a visual image, might become

I knew it was a robin because I heard its cheerful song, an auditory image. Or again,

I knew it was a robin because I felt my heart swell with spring, would be a good kinesthetic image, because it has many emotional associations.

You could even put all three of these descriptions together in a single statement:

I knew it was a robin because I felt my heart swell with the joy of spring when I heard its cheerful song, and saw the flash of its red breast against the green grass.

That's embellished a bit from the original blunt statements, but you get the point. You've communicated on all levels to your entire audience, not just a part of it. Everyone will get the message.

Focus on sensory descriptions to bring your stories to life. What can I expect to hear? See? Feel? Be my eyes, my ears, and my heart. The most compelling descriptions recreate for your audience the sensations you felt. Others fall short when they fail to touch our senses.

Quality is more important than quantity. Many a good idea has been smothered by someone's choice of words.

Your success in communication lies in your ability to get others to believe you have something they want. Excellent marketers, politicians, and salespeople know the best way to do this is to get you to experience their proposals in your mind. They do this by speaking to your senses. This involves choosing better-quality words.

Consider what Sigmund Freud has to say about words: "Words have a magical power. They can bring either the greatest happiness or deepest despair; they can transfer knowledge from teacher to student; words can enable the orator to sway his audience and dictate its decision. Words are capable of arousing the strongest emotions and promoting all men's actions."

CHOOSE YOUR WORDS CAREFULLY

Does the other person care if you heard them? "I *hear* you" is an overused phrase. I'm tired of it. My response (mentally) is, "So what!"

"Do you *see* what I mean? Do you *feel* the same way?" Try to respond to the appropriate sense of your listener.

— **Robert**

SHARPSHOOTERS

Cruelty, like every other vice, requires no motive outside itself; it only requires opportunity.
— GEORGE ELIOT

True humor does not include sarcasm, invalid irony, sardonicism, innuendo, or any other form of cruelty. When these things are raised to a high point they can become wit. But as James Thurber once noted, we North Americans (unlike the French and English) have not been much good at it since the days of Benjamin Franklin. Mr. Thurber must have been talking about Sharpshooters — skilled markspeople who attack from the concealment of sarcasm, innuendo, and twisted humor.

In her *Letters, 1931–1966* (published in 1984), Dominican-born English novelist Jean Rhys gives the perfect description of a sharpshooting environment: "I think that the desire to be cruel and to hurt (with words because any other way might be dangerous to ourself) is part of human nature. Parties are battles (most parties), a conversation is a duel (often). Everybody's trying to hurt first, to get in the dig that will make him or her feel superior, feel triumph."

You can beat the Sharpshooter at his or her own game. Here's how:

1. Remain calm, focused, and in control. You've heard this before.
2. Surface the attack — even if in public — by holding eye contact and reflecting the comments back.
3. Question the meaning. "I'm not sure I understand what you mean."
4. Recognize that this person is looking for attention. For the Sharpshooter, any attention is better than no attention. If you can, give the Expressives a chance to speak before they become Sharpshooters.
5. Focus on reality and insist, "I need you to confine your comments to the issues at hand."

LOOK AT ME!

Not all people will want to needle you. Some don't pay that much attention.

Remember the class clown? He wanted attention. So does the Sharpshooter. When he picks on you, the others around you come to life. They're glad it's you and not them. If it's important enough, say something. If it's not, ignore it. Only you know what's appropriate in the situation.

— Robert

SILENT
PARTNERS

A silent mouth is melodious.
— IRISH PROVERB

Silence is golden — or is it? Silence doesn't mean agreement; it means your partner hasn't spoken. When a silent partner refuses to speak, it's difficult for you to know what he intends to do (if anything). He may need more information, or he may be using his silence to control you.

How to handle unwanted silence:

— Ask open, specific questions — be persistent
— Expect an answer — use silence yourself
— Question your partner's silence — use humor
— Give your partner time to respond (overnight or in writing) — but set time limits
— State the importance of having to respond, as well as the consequences if your partner doesn't
— Ask if silence means agreement
— State the opposite of what you think your partner wants as a means to egg him or her on to respond.

USE SILENCE AS A TOOL

Once, while in a meeting, someone blurted out something embarrassing from my past. This person was agitated over my proposal and wanted me to appear foolish in front of the group.

I caught my breath, established eye contact, and asked, "How does that relate to my proposal?" I then waited in silence. It was important that I say nothing until my accuser responded. The person couldn't make a connection between the two.

My opponent had wanted to put me on the spot. When I requested justification for the comment and then waited for a response, the person became uncomfortable. Had I defended or denied the accusation, I would have given validity to the damaging statement and provided entertainment for the others in the room. I was able to turn around what could have been at best an interesting sideshow.

— Robert

SMALL TALK

In the world of small, nothing is insignificant.
— ENGLISH PROVERB

Small talk in North America is often regarded as insignificant, especially when it comes to business. Our whole attitude is to get to the point as quickly as possible, waste as little time as possible, and get the deal done and signed. Maybe we should rethink our position about the value of small talk.

In other cultures, no amount of business could be conducted without a suitable and frequently extensive amount of "getting-to-know-you" time. In Japan, for instance, the cultural overtones attached to small talk in business often determine whether or not the company you want to deal with will, in fact, do business with you. Extensive periods of pre-business discussion attempt to determine your attitudes about everything from art to zoology. If your responses are not judged sufficiently "civilized," business discussions may be delayed or even canceled.

While we may not always want to import such practices into our own culture, perhaps we should pay more attention to the niceties of determining the character and characteristics of our partners.

While small talk should remain small, it shouldn't be ignored.

Pay a sincere compliment, comment on the latest local sports team, or mention a common interest. It's all relevant to opening up the conversation. When the time is right, transition into the topic of business. How long does it take? That depends on you, your partner, and the urgency of your business.

DON'T RUSH THE IMPORTANT THINGS

The following lesson has been made clear to me on numerous occasions, but this one incident sticks out in my mind.

One time, while trying to close a contract with a client, I rushed into "business" too quickly. The client wasn't ready and I didn't get the contract.

Sometime later, I met the same client at a networking function. She asked how business was going and I answered. She said she had wished we could have worked together, but that I had seemed too anxious to get on with it while she had wanted to make sure I would have been a good fit. Unfortunately, I seemed to be rushing her.

I learned a valuable lesson. Not everyone is as anxious (or as patient) as you might be. Slow down or speed up. The choice is always theirs.

— Robert

SOFTENERS

*Let us always meet each other with a smile, for the
smile is the beginning of love.*
— MOTHER TERESA

Attention is part of the *HEART* approach to active listening. (The "A" in *HEART* stands for *Ask questions and attend.*) Paying attention is a good way to get your partner engaged in the conversation. One of the best ways of remembering to "attend" is to use the *SOFTENERS* mnemonic.

S *mile*
O *pen your body posture*
F *orward lean*
T *ouch*
E *ye contact*
N *odding*
E *ncouragement* — ask questions, use supportive vocalizations
R *eframing* — ask yourself "How would I feel if that was me?"
S *pace*

Nothing invites someone to open up and talk like a full, genuine smile. Even before we speak, a smile says, "I'm glad you're here. I'm looking forward to this. I accept you as my equal." Then smile again when you reach agreement.

An open body posture is an invitation to talk. Sit or stand facing your partner, with your arms and legs uncrossed.

Lean forward. This sends the message that you're paying attention and value what your partner has to say. Your body posture should be relaxed, interested, and alert.

Touch forms a powerful connection, but be careful. Touching is sometimes a "touchy" subject in today's world. It can be misunderstood, and even open you to litigation. Shaking hands with both men and women is acceptable. Anything else requires a closer relationship and special care.

Direct eye contact is expected, and encourages the speaker to say more. But excessive eye contact can also be seen as aggressive. A good policy is to "explore" your partner's face with your eyes. Look him or her in the eye, then move to the cheeks, chin, then back to the eye. It's a more friendly form of eye contact and gives the impression of interest.

Nodding, as well as other gestures that encourage your partner, communicates interest and acknowledgment. Shaking your head or having a puzzled look indicates confusion.

Encourage your partner with supportive vocalizations and put yourself in her place by reframing her actions. Ask yourself, "What would I have done if I was in that situation?" Reframing is trying to find your partner's positive intention. Rather than judging it, try to determine what her intention was.

Keep the proper distance between you and your partner. Space creates comfort and acceptance (see *Comfort Zone*). About arm's reach, or two to four feet, is an acceptable space in North America for communication. Anything closer is too intimate; anything further away is too distant. This distance varies widely between cultures and you may need to take special consideration of these differences.

PUTTING IT ALL TOGETHER

Have you ever noticed how quickly dogs make friends? They run up smiling and wagging their tails. This is the *long-lost-friend* approach to greeting someone, and it works magic. Use it for work *or* pleasure.

Smile . . . a big, warm, inviting smile . . . as though your partner is, indeed, a long-lost friend. Face the person directly and move quickly to a position within arm's length. Offer your hand in greeting while leaning in toward him or her. If you don't know the person, introduce yourself. Ask your partner's name. Exchange pleasantries . . . and wait to see if he or she moves closer.

— **Robert**

STATE
OF MIND

*I cannot escape the objection that there is no state
of mind, however simple, that does not change every
moment.*
— HENRI BERGSON

It's sometimes difficult to judge your partner's state of
mind, but it's something you must determine before you attempt communication. In the right state of mind, things will generally go easily; in the
wrong state, you may never connect.

Here are things to look for to gauge your partner's state of mind:

1. Is your partner relaxed or tense? (You may need to aid relaxation if the
   answer is "tense.")
2. Is your partner hurried or rushed? (If the answer is "hurried," it's not
   a good time to get involved in a thought-provoking conversation.)
3. Does your partner appear preoccupied? (Focus on whatever is on his
   mind first.)
4. Is your partner in silent mode? Silence is a particularly interesting state.
   Most find silence distressing and rush to fill silent gaps. Learn to
   become comfortable with silence, because it is a powerful tool.
   - Silence draws attention to something, emphasizing a point

- Silence often draws others out to volunteer information
- Silence creates tension
- Silence following a request can powerfully display your seriousness

IS THIS THE RIGHT TIME AND PLACE?

Isn't it aggravating how little value others place on your time? You're busy. You're working on a deadline. You have other concerns on your mind. Do they care? Hardly! Hear this person telling me about his problem! Can't he see I have my own? Reverse the above roles. Try to understand what this person needs from you and ask yourself, "Is this the right time and place?"

— **Robert**

SUBORDINATES

Her talent lay exclusively in seeing that other people employed theirs.
— JOSEPHINE TEY

You're paid to get things done — not necessarily to do them. How effectively you do that will depend on how effectively you communicate what you want accomplished to the people who will be accomplishing them.

Follow these guidelines when communicating with subordinates.

1. **Use formal and informal channels.** Use the grapevine, say it face to face, make formal announcements, write about it in the newsletter, publish it, send emails. Get the picture?
2. **Create a sense of urgency and expectancy.** People procrastinate. If it's old news, they will ignore it. If it's not urgent, they'll put it on the back burner. Let them know it's important and give them a deadline. Let them know what you expect and tell them you have high expectations they will complete it successfully.
3. **Explain yourself fully, demonstrate how if necessary, ask if they have questions, and observe them do it if you're unsure.** These are the four

steps required to successfully show and tell someone how to do something.

4. **Focus on desired outcomes and reasons why.** This eliminates misunderstanding about the end product or service. If they know what they're attempting to accomplish and what the finished product or service will look like, then they'll know when there are problems. By telling them why it's important to them, or to you, you'll help them appreciate the importance of their work.

5. **Involve them in the decision-making process.** Ask lots of questions. Be open to alternative approaches if they are experienced. Explain what you can and cannot do. Get them to make suggestions and then explain whether you can or cannot do that. Then allow them to make the decision from your list of can-do's.

6. **Clarify their level of authority, restrictions, reporting requirements, regulations, deadlines, and resources.** Make sure they know when to report back to you, the budget, who reports to whom when the project's done, and so on.

7. **Provide regular feedback and support.** Don't abandon them. Let them know you're there to support them and to help them if they have problems.

DON'T SHOOT THE MESSENGER

I once scolded an employee for telling me how to run my business. She never again offered suggestions. As a matter of course, you will get to hear some pretty poor suggestions from subordinates. You can't put them down, however. You need to explain why it's not appropriate for you to act on what they say. If you don't, they'll stop coming to you. Those people on the line are your people. They deserve respect.

The secret is developing superior people skills.

— Robert

TALKERS

But far more numerous was the herd of such
Who think too little and who talk too much.
— JOHN DRYDEN

The water cooler is a place to get water — and the latest gossip. Sometimes it's impossible to pull yourself away from the conversation, unless you do the following.

End conversations this way:

— Interrupt regularly in a nice way to ask specific questions about what your partner is talking about. This breaks the flow. If this doesn't work by itself, go to the next step.

— Get your partner's attention (use his name), then summarize what he's said to bring completion.

— Explain what you have to do.

— Thank your partner for sharing with you, using a downward inflection in your voice.

— Use mismatching — use different posture and eye contact than your partner to bring communication to a close.

Of course, the other way to end a conversation is simply to tell them you're busy and have to go . . .

BEAT A STRATEGIC RETREAT
There's something to be said for egotistical people — and they're usually the ones saying it! Once, while listening to someone tell me for the umpteenth time how wonderful he was, I excused myself and went to the washroom. Whatever works . . .

— **Robert**

TIME DIFFERENCES

*You need to know what time frame someone's in —
past, present, or future — to communicate with them.*
— ROBERT

In the movie *Back to the Future,* Michael J. Fox traveled through time in a futuristic DeLorean car. The chaos of seeing the past, present, and future simultaneously in the movie created an entertaining story.

As unlikely as it seems, many people exist mentally in the past, the present, or the future — and you had better be in the same time frame if your goal is mutual understanding.

For instance, you are trying to explain to a colleague or subordinate about some changes that are about to take place (future) in your company. Your colleague keeps repeating, "But we never used to do it that way (past)." You have to get your colleague to move from the past to the future by saying something like, "Can you imagine, for a moment, what these new changes will (future) bring about? No more carrying heavy cartons, for instance. No more trying to get at the bottom carton in a stack of ten." The moment your colleague responds, "I think I would like (future conditional) that," you've got him. He is now anticipating how the changes will react to his benefit.

It works the other way, too. Imagine the colleague whose vision is constantly fixed on future dreams when you want to talk about present difficulties or projects. You've got to get the person out of the future and into the present to communicate effectively.

It's really as simple as recognizing the past, present, and future tense in what your partner says. You can't focus on the future ("We'd like to," "We will") if your partner is stuck in the past ("We used to," "We did"). You must both have the same time reference.

You also need to ask yourself whether your partner is focused on the short, medium, or long term. Think about how your outcome will fit in with her goal orientation. Discover where the time reference lies, go there verbally with her, and then slowly move her into the time frame you want her to focus on.

TIME'S A TRICKSTER

Time may be a great healer, but it's no beauty specialist. A woman once exclaimed to her husband that she didn't look anything like she used to. Her husband agreed but replied, "No dear, you don't. Fortunately for me, you look better."

— Robert

|TONE

The melting voice through mazes running;
Untwisting all the chains that tie
The hidden soul of harmony.
— JOHN MILTON

The "T" in *HEART* stands for *Tone*. Does your partner's tone of voice support his thoughts, feelings, and expectations? How convinced are you about his conviction in what he's saying?

Recall that tone and body language can account for 60 to 90 percent of a person's meaning. Understanding comes from the person's intended meanings. When you're in doubt about a message, question tone or body language.

For instance, recall someone saying, "I'm interested in what you're saying" with a note of sarcasm in her voice. You might reflect, "You say you're interested but your tone leads me to think otherwise. Which is it?"

When you understand your partner's thoughts, feelings, and expectations, you are in a better position to state yours (see *FETA*).

SHOULD I BELIEVE YOU?

I was having renovations done at my home. Ken, the contractor, said he'd be there Monday at 9 a.m. Something inside me said, "Good luck." He never showed up. When there's conflict between the tone of someone's voice and that person's words, believe the tone.

— **Robert**

|TOPICS

*A journey of a thousand miles begins with but a
single step.*
— Zen PROVERB

Getting started is probably the hardest thing to accomplish in face-to-face communication, especially if the individual you're facing is a complete stranger. Emily Post used to say, "Ideal conversation must be an exchange of thought, and not, as many of those who worry most about their shortcomings believe, an eloquent exhibition of wit or oratory." You need a topic or a subject to get that communication going.

What about the weather? Nature affects us all. If it's winter and we've just experienced a major snowfall, it can lead to any number of "narrow escape" stories, as well as opening up other topics of interest. In short, the idea of a defined topic of interest is to get the other person talking. There are lots of ways to do this, but here are the five best.

1. Pleasantries and compliments — *if authentic* — are great openers.
2. Be up on trends, important issues, the recent news, sports, and local events. Use them to break the ice.
3. Ask a direct question. "What is your main interest in life outside of

business?" You'd be amazed at some of the answers you get, all of which are guaranteed good starters. Be curious. Find out what's important to your partner.

4. Involve your partner in discovering what he knows about the topic. When you do this, you accomplish three goals.

   • You discover what he knows
   • You learn what he doesn't know, so you can train him
   • You keep him mentally involved and connected

5. Recall something from the conversation earlier. It's even better if you can call it back in her own words. You might only do it as a passing comment. This forms a real bond and shows you've been listening to what she has to say. Use supportive statements such as, "That's very interesting," or "How did you ever come up with such a good idea?" or "I'm curious . . . tell me more."

LIKE WATCHING A FLOWER OPEN . . .

My friend Gail is an absolute genius at making contact with people she knows nothing about. She can take the most unimaginative, tongue-tied, shy person, and by asking simple questions she can find out what lies close to that person's heart. Once she has found that topic, she works at it until the person begins to open up.

Once she starts, she never gives up . . . and I can tell you it is just like watching a video of a flower opening once she gets the person going. I remember one instance in which she went to work on a particularly reclusive fellow. After 20 minutes' conversation, that gentleman thought she could walk on water. Every time I ran into him after that, he asked about Gail. She had really found a way to his heart.

— **Robert**

TOXIC
RELATIONSHIPS

We didn't have a relationship,
we had a personality clash.
— ALICE MOLLOY

Certain personality combinations are naturally toxic, and there's not much you can do about it except to recognize and accommodate it. Sometimes that's easier said than done, because if people can't — at least temporarily — overcome their mutual antagonisms, you may be in for a roller-coaster ride of a relationship.

Here are some examples of potentially problematic communication partners:

- The Driver and the Expressive don't get along because they both want control. Drivers don't tend to get along with each other for the same reason.
- The Amiable and the Driver have difficulty. The Driver's direct approach and lack of concern for feelings upsets the Amiable. The Driver also can't understand the Amiable's indecisiveness.
- The Expressive and the Analytical also have trouble. The Analytical

wants the details, while the Expressive is interested only in the big picture.

So who gets along, then?

— Typically, the Driver and the Analytical get along because of their task focus.
— The Amiable and the Expressive get along because of their relationship orientation.
— The Amiable also accommodates well with the Analytical, and they get along well as a result.

Under stress, however, certain additional tendencies appear in each of the four personality types. Each will behave in the pattern that demonstrates their worst characteristics, or even more baffling, they may shift into another personality type and display those weaknesses.

— The Analytical may shift to the Amiable pattern.
— The Amiable may shift to the Expressive pattern.
— The Expressive may shift to the Driver pattern.
— The Driver may shift to the Analytical pattern.

For more information see *Differences*, as well as sections on the individual personality types.

RELATIONSHIPS: DISCOVER THE UNDERLYING PROBLEM

Relationships are about the only things that seem impossible these days. Everything else makes sense.

Opposite personalities attract each other, then drive each other crazy. People like people who are like themselves, but then they get bored. People argue over right and wrong, good and bad, what's better and what's not.

People are different, not difficult. Appreciate differences. Focus on the issues and allow everyone to bring their strengths into the discussion.

I have struggled with the need for details for a long time — not because they aren't necessary, because they certainly are. It's just that I prefer to get the essential facts and then get going. My medical training taught me the value of uncovering the underlying problem before rushing in to treat symptoms. There's a time to act and a time to research. The art is in knowing when these times are.

— **Robert**

UNDERSTANDING

Understanding is your reward for listening.
— ROBERT

Understanding is the process of learning your partner's perceptions so you share his or her meaning. You don't have to accept it, but by being open-minded you can, at least for a moment, enter into your partner's world and share it as this person sees it.

Understanding isn't a tangible thing . . . it's intangible. It can't be seen, heard, or felt. It has to be received, much like a satellite dish receives a signal. First, the dish must be adjusted to face the satellite. Only then can a message be received.

Communication is the sharing of thoughts, feelings, and expectations — even in difficult situations. All are valid. Sharing means listening for your partner's thoughts, feelings, and expectations while willingly stating yours in an assertive manner.

Passive communicators merely listen, while aggressive communicators speak without listening. Assertive communicators do both. This takes high self-esteem, self-awareness, self-confidence, and empathy, but it will lead to understanding.

Understanding is the removal of distortions and the mental transformation of words, sounds, and images into shared meaning. You don't have to like or agree with the speaker, but you do need to receive what he has to say and mentally transform his message before you can evaluate it accurately and respond properly.

When you speak, you learn what you know. When you listen, you learn what your partner knows. When you ask questions, you probe for understanding.

UNDERSTAND BEFORE REACTING

Carl Jung once said, "Everything that irritates us about others can lead us to an understanding of ourselves."

I was frustrated by Ted's lack of enthusiasm. I had admired his tenacity and drive in the past but he didn't seem to care much about anything anymore. Later that year Ted was diagnosed with leukemia. While this is an extreme example, it highlights the fact that we often don't know the full story. Only occasionally do we discover the reasons behind the actions.

The more you know, the more you understand.

— Robert

VALUES

The fact that man knows right from wrong proves his intellectual superiority to the other creatures, but the fact that he can do wrong proves his moral inferiority to any creatures that cannot.
— MARK TWAIN

Colin Powell once said that the greatest power you have comes from your character. Your character is strengthened or weakened by your values. Values are what you consistently demonstrate to be true for you, not what you *say* is true for you.

Knowing your four or five key values will simplify your life. Decisions will be easier for you. When someone upsets you, you'll know which value they're colliding with, and when you have a difficult decision to make, the person will still respect you even though she may not have liked your decision.

Here's how to determine your important values. Answer these questions. Reflect on them. Look for patterns and similarities.

— What are the five things most important to you about being a good friend?
— What are the five things most important to you about being a good co-worker?

— What are the five things most important to you about being a good family person?

— Think of relationships in which things went well — answer why.

— Think of relationships in which things went poorly — answer why.

WE'RE WATCHING

Our children watch and learn from everything we do. Do you tell them not to lie, yet when someone calls for you, do you tell them to say you're not home? Do you say you're concerned about something and then do nothing about it? Do you tell them not to say bad things about playmates, and then proceed to quietly badmouth the neighbors? What do you think they are really learning?

— **Robert**

VISUAL WORDS

The difference between the almost right word and the right word is really a large matter — 'tis the difference between the lightning-bug and the lightning.
— MARK TWAIN

As we discuss in *Sensory Words,* different types of people express themselves in — and respond to — different types of words, depending on the way they perceive the world around them. Visual people relate to the world through their eyes. You can recognize visual people by their use of words such as the following, and you can use words like these to get your ideas across to them.

An eyeful	Foresee	It appears
Blind spot	Hazy	It colors the results
Crystal clear	Hide	Look
Dark	I see what you mean	Looks like
Diagram	I'm looking closely	Mental image
Dim view	Illusion	Mental picture
Eye-to-eye	Imagination	Mind's eye
Focus	In view of	Naked eye
Foggy	Inspect	Photographic memory

Pretty as a picture	See to it	Tunnel vision
Preview	Shine	Vision
Reflect	Show	Watch
Scan	Show me	You'll look back and
Scene	Take a peek	Horizon

WATCH WHAT YOU'RE SAYING!

It's better to *look* where you're going than to *see* where you've been. You will not recognize the value of suiting your choice in words to your partner's if you don't do it. Of course, these words wouldn't *ring a bell* for an auditory person, and a kinesthetic person would have trouble *grasping* your meaning.

— **Robert**

VOICE MATCHING

When two people sing in tune, it's hard to sing separately.

— ENGLISH PROVERB

There's no right or wrong way to speak, but unconsciously you're drawn to the person who speaks as you do. When you match vocal qualities with your partner, you're automatically drawn closer to each other. It's one of the most effective ways to connect.

To practice the technique consciously, try to match the rate, tone, volume, and rhythm of your partner's voice. Rates can be fast or slow, tones can be high or low, volume can be soft or loud, and rhythm can be fluid or syncopated.

It's not necessary to match your partner's speech pattern exactly — only to come close.

Don't make dramatic changes in your own voice. Simply move in the direction of your partner's. Speed your voice up or slow it down a notch to match. Interject pauses if your partner reflects a lot. Your partner probably won't even know you're copying her. That's because she's not accustomed to hearing her own voice. Our voices resonate through our bodies and sound different to us than they do on a recording, for instance.

The voice "feels" different than it "sounds."

On the telephone, words and vocal qualities are the *only* way to connect with your partner. You need to pick up the energy level in your voice, because you have lost the visual effect of body language. For best results, be enthusiastic and upbeat. Get to the point quickly. Make sure your partner knows who's speaking and why you're calling. Ask if it's a good time to call. If necessary, reschedule. Listen to your partner's tone and rate of speech, and match it.

A WHISPER IS CATCHING

A form of matching vocal qualities that we all practice is whispering. If someone whispers to you, there's a great chance you'll whisper back to him or her. No one knows why. If a man is feeling romantic, for instance, he talks to the object of his affections in a much softer voice. He doesn't become loudly vocal or strident. Couples who are planning an evening together will automatically talk more softly over dinner. Everyone does it.

— Peter

VOLCANOES

When the habitually even-tempered suddenly fly into a passion, that explosion is apt to be more impressive than the outburst of the most violent among us.
— MARGERY ALLINGHAM

We've all met difficult characters. They can't be avoided, so we have to deal with them. Here are some suggestions on dealing with one of the better-known types: the Volcano.

In the sketch "Gertrude the Governess, or Simple Seventeen" from his *Nonsense Novels,* published in 1911, Stephen Leacock has the last word on this character. "Lord Ronald said nothing; he flung himself from the room, flung himself upon his horse and rode madly off in all directions."

Volcanoes are individuals who feel frustrated and exasperated, and don't know which way to turn. Volcanoes differ from Tyrants by virtue of the fact that they rarely display this behavior. You expect this behavior from a Tyrant, but not a Volcano. Chances are the Volcano is normally very nice and giving. In fact, this is why he or she is so upset. Volcanoes give and give and give — without anyone paying attention. They then erupt.

Here are some tips on how to deal with a Volcano:

— Allow time to vent — be patient

— Consider a time-out if you're in a meeting

— Use his name to get his attention

— Speak calmly if you're not part of the problem

— Raise your voice and energy if you are the brunt of his complaint so he feels you understand the importance of his concern — choose non-inflammatory words

— Let him know you care and that you sincerely want to talk this through

— Ask questions when he has calmed down to move him from emotional responses to logical ones

— Look for the hot button and disarm it

— When he has relaxed — and *only* after he has relaxed — state that you want to work with him but you can't tolerate that type of behavior

GOING OFF WITH A BANG!

Ethel would give and give and give of herself. She was concerned with the welfare of others. But every once in a while, she would become frustrated when she felt she was doing all the work and others were taking advantage of her. To express this frustration she would cry or scream — you never knew which it would be beforehand. One thing was for certain — she had a great memory and she'd recall in vivid detail everything she had done for you. Then, the eruption would pass as quickly and as unexpectedly as it had occurred.

Ethel, like other Volcanoes, was venting her frustration. She needed reassurance that we cared. When you encounter someone like Ethel, listen and agree if she's right. Above all, let her know you appreciate her and her contributions.

— Robert

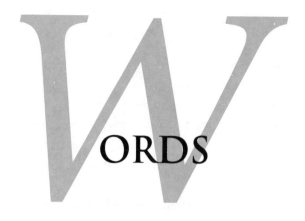

WORDS

It's wiser to choose what you say than to say what you choose.
— ROBERT

When you match someone else's words, that person feels heard and accepted. That's because the words and phrases your partner uses have a particular and specific meaning. If you substitute other words, your partner will feel you haven't quite got a grip on what's being said.

Try it. If your partner says he needs more assistance in meeting the sales quotas for the month, don't reply by asking how you can help. Ask him — and this is a subtle but important difference — "What kind of *assistance* do you need?" Pick up on the important word cues and your communication will be on target. For this reason, it's important to recognize the three broad categories of words. These are:

1. Sensory preference words
2. Key words and phrases
3. Topics and subjects

Elsewhere in this book you'll find detailed discussions of all three categories of words, as well as lists of sensory words and phrases that will clue you into the way your partner views the world — and hence, the way he or she prefers to communicate.

SAYING IT THE SAME

Your partner tells you to mind the new software because it has a tendency to freeze the hardware. Don't reply with the perfect technical counter-answer, "The new program crashes the computer?" Use his or her words. "The new software freezes the hardware?" When you say it that way, the person knows instantly that you understand. My suggestion is to use simple, specific, and short words.

— Robert

YES PEOPLE

When a diplomat says yes, he means perhaps. When he says perhaps, he means no. When he says no, he is not a diplomat.
— LORD DENNING

We've all met difficult characters. They can't be avoided, so we have to deal with them. Here are some suggestions on dealing with one of the better-known types — the Yes Person.

The Yes Person agrees with most things and follows through on very little. If they're Amiables, they don't want to hurt your feelings. If they're Expressives, they want attention and not work.

Here are some tips on how to handle Yes People:

- **Encourage disagreement.** Make it safe to disagree, do it differently, or say no.
- **Surface unrealistic commitments.** Ask about their concerns.
- **Ensure commitment through follow-up.** Don't wait until the due date — check up at specific intervals.
- **Give them an out early.** Teach them how to say "no."
- **Focus on outcomes, time commitments, and priorities.** Make sure they know what priorities they are saying "yes" to.

GET YOUR YES'S AND NO'S STRAIGHT

I had trouble saying "no." I wanted everyone to like me, so I would take on many more tasks than I could adequately handle — and, as a result, I wouldn't do as good a job as I could have done on any of them. When you say "yes" to something, you're also saying "no" to something else. I eventually adopted the philosophy of doing the most important thing I could at any given moment. Saying "no" to something permits you and others to say "yes" to more important things.

— **Robert**

RECOMMENDED READING

Alessandra, Tony, and Phil Hunsaker. *Communicating at Work*. New York: Fireside Books, 1993.

Alessandra, Tony, and Michael J. O'Conner. *The Platinum Rule*. New York: Warner Books, Inc., 1996.

Anderson, Peggy. *Great Quotes from Great Leaders*. Lombard, IL: Great Quotations, Inc., 1989.

Bender, Peter Urs. *Leadership from Within*. Toronto: Stoddart Publishing, 1997.

Bender, Peter Urs. *Secrets of Power Presentations*. Toronto: The Achievement Group, 2000.

Bender, Peter Urs, and George Torok. *Secrets of Power Marketing*. Toronto: Stoddart Publishing, 1999.

Booher, Dianna. *Communication Confidence*. Toronto: McGraw-Hill, Inc., 1994.

Bramson, Robert M. *Coping with Difficult People*. New York: Doubleday, 1983.

Brooks, Michael. *Instant Rapport*. New York: Michael Books, 1989.

Charvet, Shelle Rose. *Words that Change Minds*. Dubuque, Iowa: Kendell/Hunt Publishing Company, 1997.

Colombo, John Robert. *Famous Lasting Words*. Vancouver: Douglas & Mcintyre, 2000.

Covey, Stephen R. *The Seven Habits of Highly Effective People*. New York: Fireside, 1990.

Goleman, Daniel. *Working with Emotional Intelligence*. New York: Bantam Books, 1998.

Griessman, B. Eugene. *The Achievement Factors*. San Marcos, CA: Avant Books, 1990.

Hogan, Kevin. *Talk Your Way to the Top*. Gretna, LA: Pelican Publishing Company, Inc., 1999.

Horn, Sam. *Tongue-Fu*. New York: St. Martin's Griffen, 1996.

Laborde, Genie Z. *Influencing with Integrity*. Palo Alto, CA: Syntony Publishing, 1997.

Maggio, Rosalie. *The New Beacon Book of Quotations by Women*. Boston: Beacon Press, 1996.

Maltz, Maxwell. *PsychoCybernetics*. New York: Pocket Books, 1990.

Marshall, Lisa J., and Lucy D. Freedman. *Smart Work*. Syntax Communication Modelling Corporation, 1995.

Milo, O. Frank. *How to Get Your Point Across in 30 Seconds or Less*. New York: Simon & Schuster Inc., 1986.

Robbins, Tony. *Unlimited Power*. Toronto: Random House, 1986.

Spencer, Gerry. *How to Argue and Win Every Time*. New York: St. Martin's Press, 1995.

Webster's New Explorer Dictionary of Quotations. Springfield: Merriam-Webster, Inc., 2000.

PRESENTATIONS AND PRODUCTS

BOOKS

Secrets of Face-to-Face Communication
Secrets of Power Marketing
Secrets of Power Presentations
Leadership from Within

AUDIOTAPES

Secrets of Power Marketing
2-audiotape set
Secrets of Power Presentations
4-audiotape set (includes a 56-page workbook)

For single orders of books and tapes
call toll-free 1-800-668-9372

PRESENTATIONS

To liven up your next meeting or convention
with an entertaining speaker
contact Bender or Tracz directly:

Peter Urs Bender
108–150 Palmdale Drive
Toronto, ON M1T 3M7
416-491-6690
www.PeterUrsBender.com

Dr. Robert Tracz
194–283 Wilson Street E.
Ancaster, ON L9G 2B8
905-304-8435
www.RobertTracz.com

www.SecretsofFacetoFaceCommunication.com